Doughnut Recipes

A Doughnut Cookbook with Delicious Doughnut Recipes

By
BookSumo Press

Published by
http://www.booksumo.com

ENJOY THE RECIPES?

KEEP ON COOKING
WITH 6 MORE FREE COOKBOOKS!

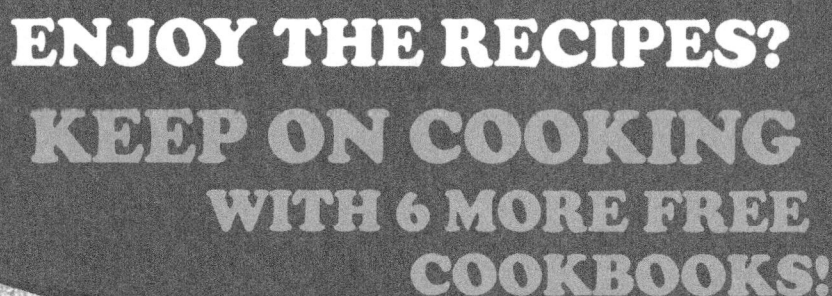

Visit our website and simply enter your email address to join the club and receive your 6 cookbooks.

http://booksumo.com/magnet

LEGAL NOTES

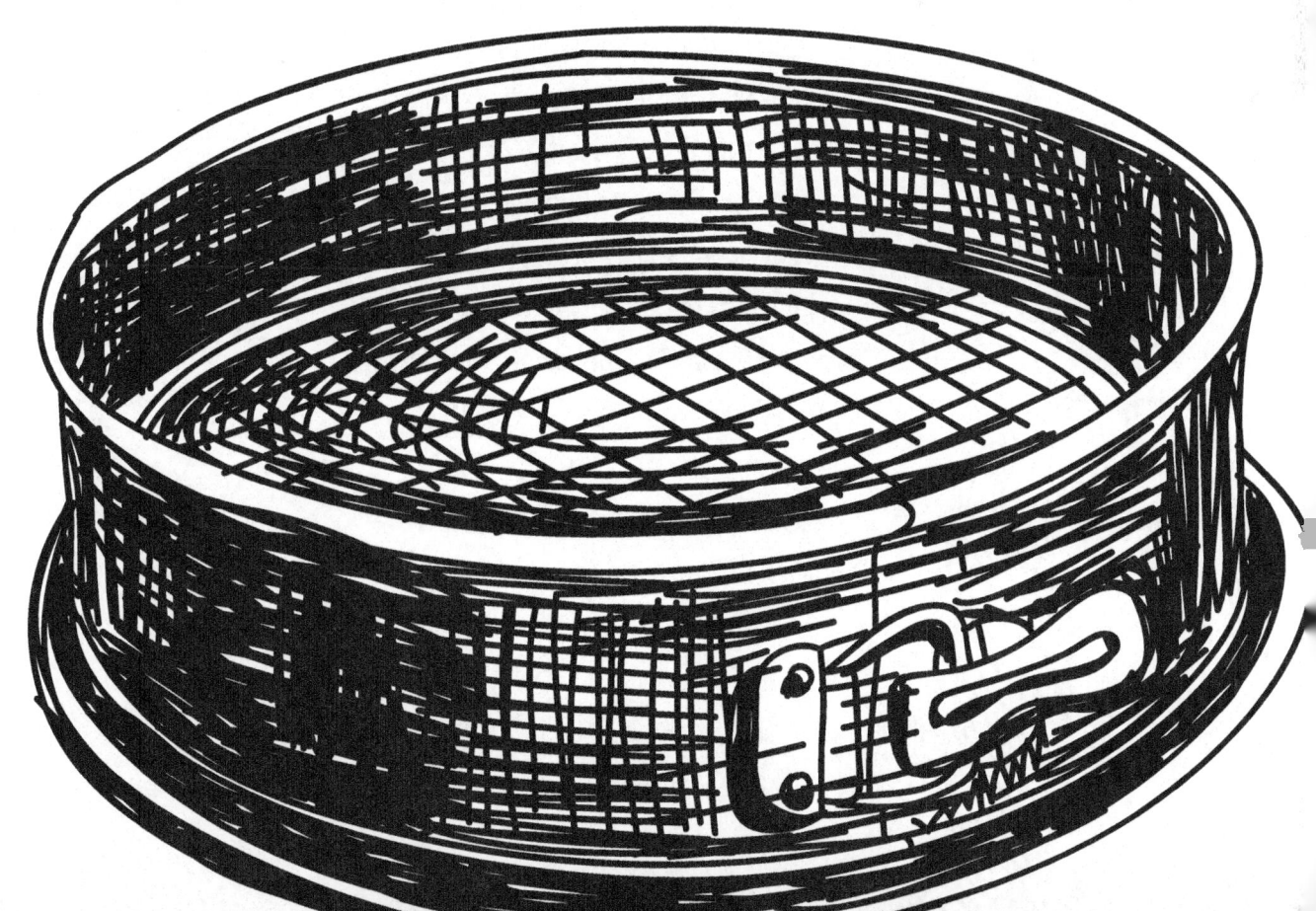

Table of Contents

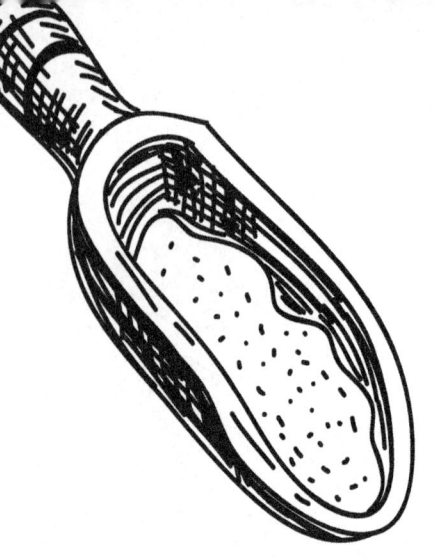

Banana
Brown Sugar Donuts

Prep Time: 15 mins
Total Time: 23 mins

Servings per Recipe: 22
Calories	102.7
Fat	0.8g
Cholesterol	0.0mg
Sodium	69.7mg
Carbohydrates	22.5g
Protein	1.8g

Ingredients

2 medium bananas
2 egg whites
1 tbsp vegetable oil
1 C. packed light brown sugar
1 1/2 C. all-purpose flour
3/4 C. whole grain wheat flour
2 tsp baking powder

1/2 tsp baking soda
1 tsp vanilla extract
1 tbsp sugar
1 tsp ground cinnamon

Directions

1. Set your oven to 425 degrees F before doing anything else and grease a baking sheet.
2. In a bowl, add the oil, egg whites, sugar and bananas and beat until well combined.
3. Add flours, baking soda, baking powder, cinnamon and vanilla and mix until well combined.
4. Keep aside for about 5 minutes.
5. With a tbsp, place the dough onto the prepared baking sheet and with a spatula, press slightly.
6. Then, with the cap of a bottle, cut a hole in the center of each doughnut.
7. Cook in the oven for about 6-10 minutes.
8. Enjoy warm.

PRE-COLONIAL
Donuts

Prep Time: 10 mins
Total Time: 20 mins

Servings per Recipe: 1 batch
Calories   236.8
Fat   4.9 g
Cholesterol   37.7 mg
Sodium   372.8 mg
Carbohydrates   42.7 g
Protein   5.2 g

Ingredients
1 C. sugar
4 tsp baking powder
1 1/2 tsp salt
1/2 tsp nutmeg
2 eggs
1/4 C. unsalted butter, melted
1 C. milk
4 C. flour
oil

cinnamon sugar

Directions
1. In a bowl, add the sugar, baking powder, nutmeg and salt and mix well.
2. Add the melted butter, milk and eggs and beat until well combined.
3. Add 3 C. of the flour and beat until well combined.
4. Add 1 C. of the flour and beat until a soft and sticky but firm dough forms.
5. With a plastic wrap, cover the dough and place in the fridge for about 2 hours.
6. Divide the dough into 2 portions.
7. Place the dough portions onto a floured surface and roll each into 1/2-inch thickness.
8. With a doughnut cutter, cut the circles from each dough portion.
9. With the cap of a bottle, cut a hole in the center of each doughnut.
10. In a deep skillet, add about 1-inch of oil and cook until its temperature reaches to 360 degrees F.
11. Place the doughnuts in batches and cook for about 2-3 minutes, flipping occasionally.
12. With a slotted spoon, transfer the doughnuts onto a paper towel-lined plate to drain.
13. Coat with the cinnamon sugar and enjoy.

My First
Spudnut

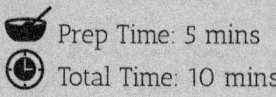 Prep Time: 5 mins

Total Time: 10 mins

Servings per Recipe: 4

Calories	308.4
Fat	7.3g
Cholesterol	61.4mg
Sodium	223.0mg
Carbohydrates	52.6g
Protein	7.3g

Ingredients

1/2 C. potato, mashed with milk and butter
1 egg, beaten
1/2 C. sour cream
1/4 C. sugar
1/2 tsp vanilla extract
1 1/2 C. all-purpose flour

1/2 tsp baking soda
1/4 tsp baking powder
cooking oil
confectioners' sugar

Directions

1. In a bowl, add the flour, baking soda and baking powder and mi well.
2. Add the flour mixture and mix until well combined.
3. Add the flour mixture and mix until well combined.
4. In a deep skillet, add the oil and cook until its temperature reaches to 375 degrees F.
5. Add the doughnuts in batches and cook for about 2 minutes, flipping once half way through.
6. With a slotted spoon, transfer the doughnuts onto a paper towel-lined plate to drain.
7. Coat the warm doughnuts with the sugar and enjoy.

PARISIAN
Cinnamon Donuts

Prep Time: 15 mins
Total Time: 45 mins

Servings per Recipe: 14
Calories	172.4
Fat	9.7g
Cholesterol	14.5mg
Sodium	214.1mg
Carbohydrates	19.4g
Protein	2.2g

Ingredients

5 tbsp margarine
1/2 C. sugar
1 egg
1 1/2 C. flour
2 1/4 tsp baking powder
1/4 tsp salt
1/2 tsp nutmeg
1/2 C. milk
6 tbsp margarine, melted

3 tsp cinnamon
1 tbsp sugar

Directions

1. Set your oven to 350 degrees F before doing anything else and grease 14 cups of muffin pans.
2. In a bowl, add the flour, baking powder, nutmeg and salt and mix well.
3. In another bowl, add the sugar and margarine and beat until creamy.
4. Add the egg and beat until well combined.
5. Add the flour mixture, alternating with the milk and mix until just combined.
6. Place the mixture into the prepared muffin cups about half way full.
7. Cook in the oven for about 20 - 25 minutes.
8. Remove from the oven.
9. Then, immediately, remove the doughnuts from the pan.
10. Dip each doughnut into margarine and then, coat with the cinnamon sugar.

Sweet
Buttermilk Donut (Gluten Free)

Prep Time: 30 mins

Total Time: 40 mins

Servings per Recipe: 16

Calories	120.3
Fat	3.7g
Cholesterol	32.1mg
Sodium	537.2mg
Carbohydrates	20.4g
Protein	1.8g

Ingredients

2 eggs, beaten
2 C. buttermilk
1/4 C. butter, melted
5 C. gluten-free rice flour mix
1 C. sugar
1 tsp nutmeg
1/2 tsp cinnamon

2 tsp baking soda
1 tsp baking powder
2 tsp salt
2 tsp xanthan gum
1/2 C. sugar, set aside in a bowl

Directions

1. In a bowl, add the flour mix, sugar, baking soda, baking powder, xanthan gum, spices and salt and mix well.
2. In another bowl, add the butter, eggs and buttermilk and beat until well combined.
3. Add the flour mixture and gently, stir until just combined.
4. Now, with your hands, knead until a dough forms.
5. Keep aside for about 15 minutes.
6. Place the dough onto a floured surface and roll into 1/3-1/2-inch thickness.
7. With a doughnut cutter, cut the doughnuts.
8. Then, with the cap of a bottle, cut a hole in the center of each doughnut.
9. In a deep skillet, add 2-3-inch of the canola oil and cook until its temperature reaches to 375 degrees F.
10. Add the doughnuts in batches and cook until golden brown from both sides.
11. Coat the warm doughnuts with the sugar and enjoy.

DOUGHNUTS
in July

🍲 Prep Time: 3 hr
🕐 Total Time: 3 hr 30 mins

Servings per Recipe: 1
Calories	137.5
Fat	2.9g
Cholesterol	22.0mg
Sodium	101.3mg
Carbohydrates	24.8g
Protein	2.9g

Ingredients
2 C. scalded milk
1/2 C. butter
2/3 C. sugar, divided
1 tsp salt
2 tbsp yeast
4 eggs, beaten
1/4 tsp nutmeg

7 C. sifted flour
Coating
3 C. powdered sugar
1/2 tsp salt
1/2 tsp vanilla
1/2 C. cold water

Directions
1. For the glaze: in a bowl, add all the ingredients and mix until well combined.
2. Keep aside.
3. In a pan, add the hot milk and butter and mix until butter is melted completely.
4. Add 1 tsp of the sugar and salt and mix well.
5. Keep aside to cool.
6. After cooling, add the eggs, remaining sugar, 3 C. of the flour, yeast and nutmeg and mix until well combined.
7. Add the remaining flour and mix until a sticky dough forms.
8. Now, with your hands, knead for about 5 minutes.
9. Keep aside for about 1-1 1/2 hours.
10. Place the dough onto a floured surface and roll into desired thickness.
11. Cut the dough into desired sized shapes.
12. Keep aside for about 30-45 minutes.
13. In a deep skillet, add the oil and cook until its temperature reaches to 365 degrees F.
14. Add the doughnuts in batches and cook for about 2-4 minutes, flipping once half way through.
15. With a slotted spoon, transfer the doughnuts onto a paper towel-lined plate to drain.
16. Coat the warm doughnuts with the glaze and enjoy.

Florida
Buttermilk Donuts

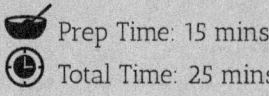 Prep Time: 15 mins

Total Time: 25 mins

Servings per Recipe: 1
Calories	165.8
Fat	3.1g
Cholesterol	0.8mg
Sodium	223.3mg
Carbohydrates	33.0g
Protein	1.6g

Ingredients

deep frying oil
7 1/2 oz. buttermilk biscuits
4 tbsp sugar
Coating
2 C. powdered sugar

1/4 C. milk
1 tsp vanilla

Directions

1. Carefully, separate the dough into 10 biscuits.
2. Then, with the cap of a bottle, cut a hole in the center of each biscuit.
3. In a deep skillet, add the oil and cook until its temperature reaches to 350 degrees F.
4. Add the doughnuts in batches and cook for about 3 minutes, flipping once half way through.
5. With a slotted spoon, transfer the doughnuts onto a paper towel-lined plate to drain.
6. Meanwhile, for the glaze: in a bowl, add the milk, powdered sugar and vanilla and mix well.
7. Coat the warm doughnuts with the sugar and then, dip into glaze.
8. Enjoy.

DONUTS
in the Bread Machine I

Prep Time: 15 mins
Total Time: 55 mins

Servings per Recipe: 1
Calories	1262.6
Fat	35.9g
Cholesterol	114.3mg
Sodium	1279.1mg
Carbohydrates	200.4g
Protein	31.9g

Ingredients
1 1/4 C. milk
1 beaten egg
1/4 C. shortening
1/4 C. sugar

1 tsp salt
3 1/2 C. white flour
1 1/2 tsp dry yeast

Directions
1. In a bread machine pan, place all the ingredients in order as suggested by the manual.
2. Select the Dough cycle and press the Start button.
3. Place the dough onto floured surface and roll into 1/2-inch thickness.
4. With a 2-1/2-inch doughnut cutter, cut the doughnuts.
5. Then, with the cap of a bottle, cut a hole in the center of each doughnut.
6. with a kitchen towel, covered the doughnuts and keep aside for about 30 minutes.
7. In a deep skillet, add the oil and cook until its temperature reaches to 375 degrees F.
8. Add the doughnuts in batches and cook until golden brown from both sides.
9. With a slotted spoon, transfer the doughnuts onto a paper towel-lined plate to drain.
10. Coat the warm doughnuts with the sugar and enjoy.

Strawberry
Jelly Donuts

Prep Time: 1 hr
Total Time: 1 hr 4 mins

Servings per Recipe: 40
Calories	124.0
Fat	2.6g
Cholesterol	10.5mg
Sodium	69.5mg
Carbohydrates	22.8g
Protein	2.3g

Ingredients

2 (1/4 oz.) envelope dry yeast
1/4 C. warm water
1 1/2 C. lukewarm milk
3/4 C. sugar
1 tsp salt
2 eggs

6 tbsp shortening
5 C. flour
oil
1 (13 1/2 oz.) jar strawberry jelly
confectioners' sugar

Directions

1. In a bowl, add the warm water and sprinkle with the yeast.
2. Keep aside for about minutes.
3. In a bowl, add the 2 C. of the flour, yeast mixture, sugar, salt, milk, shortening, sugar and eggs and with an electric mixer; beat on low speed until well combined.
4. Add the remaining flour, 1/2 C. at a time and mix until a non-sticky dough forms.
5. With your hands, knead until smooth and elastic dough forms.
6. In a greased bowl, place the dough.
7. With a plastic wrap, cover the dough and keep in a warm place for about 1 hour.
8. Place the dough onto a floured surface and roll into 1/2-inch thickness.
9. With a doughnut cutter, cut the doughnuts.
10. Keep aside until doubled in size.
11. In a deep skillet, add 4 C. of the oil and cook until its temperature reaches to 350 degrees F.
12. Add the doughnuts in batches and cook until golden brown from both sides.
13. Add the doughnuts in batches and cook for about 2-4 minutes, flipping once half way through.
14. With a slotted spoon, transfer the doughnuts onto a paper towel-lined plate to drain.
15. With a pastry injector, fill each doughnut with the jelly evenly.
16. Coat with the confectioners' sugar and enjoy.

20-MINUTE
Donut Biscuits

Prep Time: 10 mins
Total Time: 25 mins

Servings per Recipe: 10
Calories   319.5
Fat   15.0g
Cholesterol   24.4mg
Sodium   538.5mg
Carbohydrates   45.3g
Protein   2.8g

Ingredients
2 (7 1/2 oz.) packages refrigerated
buttermilk biscuits
1/2 C. butter, melted
1 C. sugar
4 tbsp cinnamon
10 tsp raspberry jam

Directions
1. Set your oven to 375 degrees F before doing anything else and grease a baking sheet.
2. In a microwave-safe bowl, add the butter and microwave for about 45 seconds.
3. In a bowl, add the cinnamon and sugar and mix well.
4. Coat the edge of a biscuit with the melted butter and then with the cinnamon sugar.
5. In the bottom of the prepared baking sheet, arrange the biscuits.
6. Now, spread about 1/2 tsp of the jam in the center of each biscuit.
7. With your finger, make a little well in the center of each biscuit.
8. Cook in the oven for about 15 minutes.
9. Enjoy warm.

Milanese Cheese Donuts

Prep Time: 15 mins

Total Time: 25 mins

Servings per Recipe: 24
Calories	43.2
Fat	1.6g
Cholesterol	13.2mg
Sodium	42.8mg
Carbohydrates	5.0g
Protein	2.0g

Ingredients

1 egg, beaten
1 tbsp sugar
1 C. all-purpose flour
3 tbsp milk
2 tsp baking powder
1 C. ricotta cheese
vegetable oil

Directions

1. In a bowl, add all the ingredients and mix until well combined.
2. In a deep skillet, add the oil and cook until heated through.
3. With a tsp, add the mixture and cook until golden brown from both sides.
4. With a slotted spoon, transfer the doughnuts onto a paper towel-lined plate to drain.
5. Dust with the powdered sugar and enjoy.

PUMPKIN
Donuts in Fall

Prep Time: 10 mins
Total Time: 20 mins

Servings per Recipe: 12
Calories   204.4
Fat   5.1g
Cholesterol   42.1mg
Sodium   245.3mg
Carbohydrates   36.3g
Protein   3.6g

Ingredients
2 C. all-purpose flour
1/2 C. packed brown sugar
1 1/2 tsp baking powder
1 1/2 tsp pumpkin pie spice
1/2 tsp salt
1/4 tsp baking soda
1/2 C. canned pumpkin
2 eggs
1/4 C. milk

1/4 C. butter, softened
Frosting
1 C. powdered sugar, sifted
1/4 tsp vanilla
4 -5 tsp milk

Directions
1. Set your oven to 375 degrees F before doing anything else and grease 2 baking sheets.
2. For the doughnuts: in a bowl, add the flour, baking powder, baking soda, brown sugar, pumpkin pie spice and salt and mix well.
3. Add the butter, milk, eggs and pumpkin and with an electric mixer, beat on low speed until well combined.
4. In a pastry bag, fitted with a large star tip with a 1/2-inch opening, place the pumpkin mixture.
5. In the bottom of each prepared baking sheets, pipe the mixture in a 3-inch circles.
6. Cook in the oven for about 10-12 minutes.
7. Remove from the oven and place the doughnuts onto a wire rack.
8. For the icing: in a bowl, add the powdered sugar and vanilla and mix well.
9. Add enough milk and mix until a glaze like icing is formed.
10. Coat the top of each doughnut with the icing and enjoy.

Amish
Donut Holes

Prep Time: 5 mins
Total Time: 15 mins

Servings per Recipe: 4
Calories	225.0
Fat	7.2g
Cholesterol	0.7mg
Sodium	318.5mg
Carbohydrates	34.7g
Protein	5.2g

Ingredients

2 tbsp vegetable oil
3 tbsp granulated sugar
1/4 C. egg substitute
1 C. all-purpose flour
1 1/2 tsp baking powder
1/4 tsp salt
4 tbsp low-fat milk

1/8 tsp nutmeg
granulated sugar
cinnamon sugar
confectioners' sugar

Directions

1. In a bowl, add the flour, sugar, baking powder, nutmeg and salt and mix well.
2. In another bowl, add the milk, oil and egg substitute and beat until well combined.
3. Add the flour mixture and mix until well combined.
4. In a deep skillet, add the oil and cook until its temperature reaches to 375 degrees F.
5. With a tsp, add the mixture and cook until golden brown from both sides.
6. With a slotted spoon, transfer the doughnut holes onto a paper towel-lined plate to drain.
7. Coat the warm doughnuts with the confectioner's sugar and enjoy.

FROSTED
Doughnuts

Prep Time: 30 mins
Total Time: 40 mins

Servings per Recipe: 1
Calories	98.5
Fat	2.6g
Cholesterol	8.1mg
Sodium	52.3mg
Carbohydrates	16.3g
Protein	2.2g

Ingredients
1 C. milk, lukewarm
1 (1/4 oz.) package yeast
1 C. lukewarm water
1/2 C. shortening
2/3 C. sugar
2 eggs, beaten
1 tsp salt
7 C. flour

Directions
1. In a bowl, add the warm water and sprinkle with the yeast.
2. Keep aside for about 10 minutes.
3. Add the milk and stir to combine
4. In another bowl, add sugar and shortening and beat until creamy.
5. Add eggs and beat until well combined.
6. Add the flour and salt, alternating with the milk mixture and mix until smooth.
7. With a plastic wrap, cover the bowl and keep aside in warm place until doubled in size.
8. Place the dough onto a floured surface and roll into 1/2-inch thickness.
9. With a doughnut cutter, cut the doughnuts.
10. Keep aside until doubled in size.
11. In a deep skillet, add the oil and cook until heated through.
12. Add the doughnuts in batches and cook until golden brown from both sides.
13. With a slotted spoon, transfer the doughnuts onto a paper towel-lined plate to drain.
14. Coat the warm doughnuts with the sugar glaze and enjoy.

No Fry
Donuts

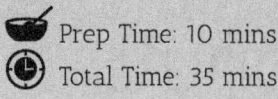 Prep Time: 10 mins

Total Time: 35 mins

Servings per Recipe: 10
Calories	284.8
Fat	12.7g
Cholesterol	31.7mg
Sodium	227.1mg
Carbohydrates	39.7g
Protein	3.5g

Ingredients
1 3/4 C. flour
1 1/2 tsp baking powder
1/2 tsp salt
1/2 tsp ground nutmeg
1/4 tsp ground cinnamon
3/4 C. sugar
1/3 C. vegetable oil

1 egg, beaten
3/4 C. low-fat milk
jam
Coating
1/4 C. butter, melted
1/3 C. sugar
1 tsp ground cinnamon

Directions
1. Set your oven to 350 degrees F before doing anything else and grease a muffin pan.
2. In a bowl, add the flour, baking powder, cinnamon, nutmeg and salt and mix well.
3. In another bowl, add the milk, oil, sugar and egg and beat until well combined.
4. Add the flour mixture and mix until just combined.
5. In the prepared muffin cups, place the mixture about 1/2 full and top each with 1 tsp of the jam.
6. Now, place the remaining mixture over the jam in each muffin cup about 3/4 of the full.
7. Cook in the oven for about 20-25 minutes.
8. Remove from the oven and keep onto the wire rack to cool in the pan for about 5 minutes.
9. Carefully, invert the muffins onto the wire rack to cool completely.
10. In a bowl, place the melted butter.
11. In another bowl, add the sugar and cinnamon and mix well.
12. Immediately, dip the tops in butter and coat with the cinnamon sugar.

BATON ROUGE
Donuts

Prep Time: 10 mins
Total Time: 35 mins

Servings per Recipe: 1
Calories	220.1
Fat	14.1g
Cholesterol	38.6mg
Sodium	213.0mg
Carbohydrates	21.4g
Protein	2.4g

Ingredients
1 1/2 C. sifted flour
1 3/4 tsp baking powder
1/2 tsp salt
1/2 tsp nutmeg
1/2 C. sugar
1/3 C. shortening
1 beaten egg
1/4 C. milk
1/2 C. grated apple

1/2 C. butter, melted
cinnamon sugar

Directions
1. Set your oven to 350 degrees F before doing anything else and grease a doughnut pan.
2. In a bowl, add the flour, sugar, baking powder, nutmeg and salt and mix well.
3. With a pastry blender, cut in the shortening.
4. Add the milk, egg and apples and mix well.
5. In the prepared doughnut pan, place the mixture about 2/3 of full.
6. Cook in the oven for about 20 - 25 minutes.
7. Coat the warm doughnuts with 1/2 C. of the melted butter and then with the cinnamon-sugar.
8. Enjoy.

Simple
Sour Donuts

Prep Time: 10 mins
Total Time: 15 mins

Servings per Recipe: 10
Calories	273.8
Fat	5.8g
Cholesterol	49.1mg
Sodium	275.7mg
Carbohydrates	49.4g
Protein	5.6g

Ingredients

1 C. sour cream
1 C. granulated sugar
2 large eggs
1 tsp baking soda
1/2 tsp salt
3 C. all-purpose flour
1/8-1/4 tsp nutmeg

1 tsp vanilla extract
icing sugar

Directions

1. In a bowl, add the flour, baking soda, nutmeg and salt and mix well.
2. In another bowl, add the sugar and sour cream and beat well.
3. Add the eggs and beat until well combined.
4. Add the flour mixture and mix well.
5. Place the dough onto a floured surface and roll into 3/4-inch thickness.
6. With a doughnut cutter, cut the doughnuts.
7. In a deep skillet, add the oil and cook until its temperature reaches to 370 degrees F.
8. Add the doughnuts in batches and cook until golden brown from both sides.
9. With a slotted spoon, transfer the doughnuts onto a paper towel-lined plate to drain.
10. Sprinkle the warm doughnuts with the icing sugar and enjoy.

A HOMESTEADER'S
Favorite

Prep Time: 20 mins
Total Time: 32 mins

Servings per Recipe: 12
Calories   214.1
Fat   3.7g
Cholesterol   0.0mg
Sodium   268.1mg
Carbohydrates   42.5g
Protein   2.8g

Ingredients

3 tbsp granulated sugar
2 1/2 tsp cinnamon, divided
2 C. all-purpose flour
1 1/2 tsp baking powder
1 1/2 tsp baking soda
1/4 tsp salt
2 large egg whites, beaten
2/3 C. packed brown sugar
1/2 C. apple butter

1/3 C. pure maple syrup
1/3 C. apple cider
1/3 C. nonfat vanilla yogurt
3 tbsp canola oil
1 tsp vanilla extract

Directions

1. Set your oven to 400 degrees F before doing anything else and grease the molds of 2 mini bundt cake pans.

2. In a bowl, add the granulated sugar and 1/2 tsp of the cinnamon and mix well.

3. In the bottom of the prepared cake molds, Place some of the cinnamon sugar evenly and shake out the excess.

4. In a bowl, add the flour, baking soda, baking powder, remaining 2 tsp of the cinnamon and salt and mix well.

5. In a second bowl, add the brown sugar, egg whites, yogurt, maple syrup, apple butter, apple cider, canola oil and vanilla extract and bet until well combined.

6. Add the flour mixture and mix until just combined.

7. In the prepared cake molds, place the mixture evenly and top with the reserved cinnamon sugar.

8. Cook in the oven for about 10-12 minutes.

9. Remove from the oven and keep onto a wire rack to cool for about 2 minutes.

10. Carefully, invert the doughnuts onto the wire rack and enjoy.

Donuts
in the Bread Machine II

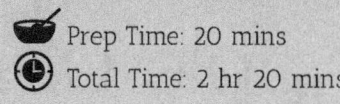 Prep Time: 20 mins

Total Time: 2 hr 20 mins

Servings per Recipe: 1

Calories	186.9
Fat	7.5g
Cholesterol	19.3mg
Sodium	98.8mg
Carbohydrates	26.9g
Protein	3.1g

Ingredients

3 medium potatoes, peeled and quartered
1 C. milk
2 eggs, well beaten
3/4 C. shortening
1/2 C. sugar
1 tsp salt

4 1/2 C. bread flour
2 1/4 tsp active dry yeast
Coating
3/4 C. sugar
1 1/4 tsp ground cinnamon
1/4 C. butter, melted

Directions

1. In a pan of the water, add the potatoes and cook until boiling.
2. Cook until cooked through.
3. Drain the potatoes, reserving 1/4 C. of the cooking water in a bowl.
4. Keep the liquid aside to cool to 70-80 degrees F.
5. With a potato masher, mash the potatoes completely and place bout 1 C. in a bowl.
6. Keep aside in room temperature to cool.
7. In bread machine pan, place the dough ingredients in order as suggested by the manual alongside 1 C. of the cooled mashed potatoes and reserved cooking water.
8. Select the Dough cycle.
9. After the completion of cycle, transfer the dough onto a lightly floured surface and roll into 1/2-inch thickness.
10. With a 2 1/2-inch doughnut cutter, cut the doughnuts.
11. In 2 greased baking sheets, arrange the doughnuts.
12. With plastic sheets, cover the baking sheets and keep aside in warm place for about 25 minutes.
13. Set your oven to 350 degrees F.
14. Cook in the oven for about 15-20 minutes.
15. Meanwhile, in a bowl, add the cinnamon and sugar and mix well.
16. Coat the warm doughnuts with the butter and the cinnamon sugar.

MOM'S EASY
Apple Donuts

Prep Time: 5 mins
Total Time: 20 mins

Servings per Recipe: 3
Calories	121.6
Fat	2.0g
Cholesterol	23.5mg
Sodium	151.0mg
Carbohydrates	22.8g
Protein	2.8g

Ingredients
3 tbsp butter, softened
3/4 C. sugar
3 eggs
1 C. applesauce
1 tsp vanilla extract
4 1/2 C. all-purpose flour
3 1/2 tsp baking powder
1 tsp salt
1/2-3/4 tsp cinnamon, ground

1/4-1/2 tsp nutmeg, ground
1/4 C. milk
oil
sugar

Directions
1. In a bowl, add the flour, baking powder, cinnamon, nutmeg and salt and mix well.
2. In another bowl, add the sugar and butter and beat until creamy.
3. Add the eggs, one at a time and beat well.
4. Add the vanilla extract and applesauce and beat until well combined.
5. Add the flour mixture, alternating with the milk and mix until a thick mixture is formed.
6. In a deep skillet, add the oil and cook until its temperature reaches to 375 degrees F.
7. With a tsp, place the mixture and cook until golden brown from both sides.
8. With a slotted spoon, transfer the doughnuts onto a paper towel-lined plate to drain.
9. Coat the warm doughnuts with the sugar and enjoy.

Japanese Donuts

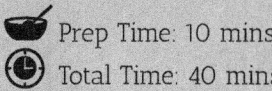 Prep Time: 10 mins

Total Time: 40 mins

Servings per Recipe: 12
Calories	317.7
Fat	2.6g
Cholesterol	72.6mg
Sodium	397.8mg
Carbohydrates	66.9g
Protein	6.9g

Ingredients

oil
4 eggs
3/4 C. milk
3/4 tsp vanilla
4 C. flour
2 C. sugar
3 1/2 tbsp baking powder

1/4 tsp salt

Directions

1. In a bowl, add the flour, baking powder, sugar and salt and mix well.
2. Now, sift the flour mixture into another bowl.
3. In another bowl, add the milk, eggs and vanilla and beat until well combined.
4. Add the flour mixture and mix until a smooth dough forms.
5. In a deep skillet, add the oil and cook until its temperature reaches to 350 degrees F.
6. With a tsp, place the mixture and cook until golden brown from both sides.
7. With a slotted spoon, transfer the doughnuts onto a paper towel-lined plate to drain.
8. Enjoy hot.

30-MINUTE
Donut Drop

Prep Time: 20 mins
Total Time: 28 mins

Servings per Recipe: 10
Calories	326.5
Fat	6.6g
Cholesterol	76.0mg
Sodium	197.1mg
Carbohydrates	59.4g
Protein	6.9g

Ingredients
1/4 C. butter, softened
1 C. sugar
2 large egg yolks, Beaten
1 large egg, Beaten
4 C. unbleached flour
2 tsp baking powder
1/4 tsp nutmeg
1/2 tsp baking soda
3/4 C. buttermilk

confectioners' sugar

Directions
1. In a bowl, add the flour, baking powder, baking soda, nutmeg and salt and mix well.
2. Now, sift the flour mixture into another bowl.
3. In another bowl, add the sugar and butter and beat until creamy.
4. Add the whole egg and egg yolks and beat until well combined.
5. Add the flour mixture, alternating with the buttermilk and mix until well combined.
6. In a deep skillet, add the oil and cook until its temperature reaches to 375 degrees F.
7. With a tsp, place the mixture and cook until golden brown from both sides.
8. With a slotted spoon, transfer the doughnuts onto a paper towel-lined plate to drain.
9. Enjoy hot.

Orange
Glazed Veggie Puffs

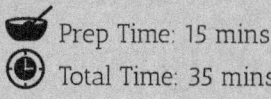 Prep Time: 15 mins

Total Time: 35 mins

Servings per Recipe: 8

Calories	478.9
Fat	5.2g
Cholesterol	56.2mg
Sodium	411.8mg
Carbohydrates	100.4g
Protein	8.0g

Ingredients

vegetable oil
2 eggs
1/2 C. brown sugar
1/2 C. white sugar
2 tbsp butter, melted
1/2 C. milk
2 tbsp cooking sherry
1 tsp vanilla
1 1/2 tsp orange zest

1 C. zucchini, shredded drained
3 1/2 C. flour
1 tbsp baking powder
3/4 tsp salt
1 tsp cinnamon
1/2 tsp nutmeg
Topping
2 C. powdered sugar
3 tbsp orange juice

Directions

1. In a bowl, add the flour, baking powder, cinnamon, nutmeg and salt and mix well.
2. In another bowl, add the eggs and beat well.
3. Add the cream and both sugars and beat until creamy.
4. Add the sherry, milk, melted butter, vanilla and orange zest and beat until well combined.
5. Add the zucchini and stir to combine.
6. Add the flour mixture and mix until just combined.
7. In a deep skillet, add the oil and cook until its temperature reaches to 370 degrees F.
8. With a tsp, add the mixture and cook until golden brown from both sides.
9. With a slotted spoon, transfer the doughnuts onto a paper towel-lined plate to drain.
10. For the glaze: in a bowl, add the powdered sugar and orange juice and beat until well combined.
11. Coat the warm doughnuts with the glaze and enjoy.

POTLUCK
Donuts

Prep Time: 1 hr
Total Time: 2 hr

Servings per Recipe: 5
Calories	80.6
Fat	1.2g
Cholesterol	8.7mg
Sodium	65.7mg
Carbohydrates	15.7g
Protein	1.7g

Ingredients
4 tbsp of melted butter
2 C. white sugar
2 eggs
2 C. milk
2 tsp cream of tartar
1 tsp baking soda
4 tsp baking powder
1/2 tsp salt
1 1/2 tsp nutmeg

1/2 tsp cinnamon
7 - 8 C. flour
sugar
oil

Directions
1. In a bowl, add the flour, baking soda, baking powder, cream of tartar, nutmeg, cinnamon and salt and mix well.
2. Now, sift the flour mixture into another bowl.
3. In another bowl, add the eggs, sugar and butter and beat until creamy.
4. Add the flour mixture, alternating with the milk and mix until well combined.
5. Place the dough onto a floured surface and roll into 1/4-inch thickness.
6. With a doughnut cutter, cut the doughnuts.
7. In a deep skillet, add the oil and cook until its temperature reaches to 365 degrees F.
8. Add the doughnuts in batches and cook until golden brown from both sides.
9. With a slotted spoon, transfer the doughnuts onto a paper towel-lined plate to drain.
10. Coat the warm doughnuts with the sugar and enjoy.

Vanilla
Crème Donuts

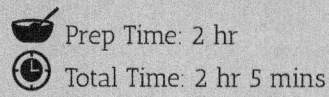 Prep Time: 2 hr

Total Time: 2 hr 5 mins

Servings per Recipe: 12
Calories   318.1
Fat   13.7g
Cholesterol   28.1mg
Sodium   146.8mg
Carbohydrates   45.1g
Protein   4.0g

Ingredients

1 (1/4 oz.) package quick-rising yeast
1/8 C. tap water, warm
3/4 C. milk, lukewarm scalded then cooled
1/4 C. sugar
1/2 tsp salt
1 egg
1/4 C. shortening

2 1/2 C. all-purpose flour
Filling
1/4 C. vegetable shortening
1/4 C. butter
1/2 tsp clear vanilla extract
2 C. sifted confectioners' sugar
1 tbsp evaporated milk

Directions

1. In a bowl, add the warm water and yeast and mix until well combined.
2. Add the egg, milk, shortening, 1 C. of the flour, sugar and salt and with an electric mixer, beat on low speed for about 30 seconds.
3. Set the speed on medium and beat for about 2 minutes.
4. Add the remaining flour and mix until smooth.
5. With a plastic wrap, cover the bowl and keep aside in warm area for about 50-60 minutes.
6. Place the dough onto a floured surface and roll into 1/2-inch thickness.
7. With a round cookie cutter, cut the doughnuts.
8. In the bottom of 2 floured baking sheets, arrange the doughnuts.
9. With a plastic wrap, cover the bowl and keep aside in warm area for about 30-40 minutes.
10. In a deep skillet, add the oil and cook until its temperature reaches to 350 degrees F.
11. Add the doughnuts in batches and cook until golden brown from both sides.

12. With a slotted spoon, transfer the doughnuts onto a paper towel-lined plate to drain.

13. Meanwhile, for the filling: in a bowl, add the shortening and butter and beat until creamy.

14. Slowly, add the sugar, 1/2 cup at a time and beat until well combined.

15. Add the milk and vanilla and beat until light and fluffy.

16. Make a small hole in the center of each cooled doughnut.

17. Fill each doughnut with the filling generously and enjoy with a dusting of the confectioners' sugar.

Italian
Boardwalk Donuts (Zeppoles)

🥣 Prep Time: 15 mins
🕐 Total Time: 25 mins

Servings per Recipe: 24
Calories   88.8
Fat   4.7g
Cholesterol   45.4mg
Sodium   63.5mg
Carbohydrates   10.2g
Protein   1.6g

Ingredients

1 vanilla bean
1/2 C. sugar
3 tbsp sugar
2 tbsp ground cinnamon
1/2 C. butter
1/4 tsp salt
1 C. water
1 C. all-purpose flour

4 eggs
olive oil

Directions

1. Open the vanilla bean lengthwise and then, with the back of a knife, scrape the seeds.
2. Ina bowl, add the vanilla bean seeds, 1/2 C. of the sugar and cinnamon and mix well.
3. In a pan, add the butter, 3 tbsp of the sugar, salt and water over medium heat and cook until boiling.
4. Remove from the heat and stir in the flour until well combined.
5. Again, place the pan over the heat and cook for about 4-5 minutes, mixing constantly.
6. Transfer the flour mixture into a bowl.
7. Add the eggs, 1 at a time and with an electric hand mixer, beat on low speed until well combined and smooth.
8. In a deep skillet, add the oil and cook until its temperature reaches to 375 degrees F.
9. With a small ice-cream scooper, add the mixture and cook for about 5 minutes, flipping once half way through.
10. With a slotted spoon, transfer the doughnuts onto a paper towel-lined plate to drain.
11. Coat the warm doughnuts with the cinnamon sugar and enjoy.

LULU'S
Little Donuts

Prep Time: 15 mins
Total Time: 45 mins

Servings per Recipe: 1
Calories	1122.5
Fat	51.7g
Cholesterol	236.3mg
Sodium	1047.7mg
Carbohydrates	151.4g
Protein	15.3g

Ingredients
1 1/2 C. all-purpose flour
3/4 C. sugar
2 tsp baking powder
1/4 tsp salt
1/4 tsp nutmeg
1 large egg
1/2 C. milk
1/2 C. melted butter
1/2 tsp vanilla

1/2 tsp ground cinnamon

Directions
1. Set your oven to 350 degrees F before doing anything else and grease cups of a mini muffin pan.
2. In a bowl, add the flour, baking powder, 1/2 C. of the sugar, nutmeg and salt and mix well.
3. In a second bowl, add the milk, egg, 1/4 C. of the melted butter and vanilla and beat until well combined.
4. Add the flour mixture and mix until just combined.
5. In the prepared muffin cups, place the mixture evenly.
6. Cook in the oven for about 15 minutes.
7. Meanwhile, in a bowl, add the cinnamon and 1/3 C. of the sugar and mix well.
8. Coat the warm doughnut tops with 3 tbsp of the melted butter.
9. Coat with the cinnamon sugar and enjoy.

34   Lulu's Little Donuts

Hot
Vanilla Donuts

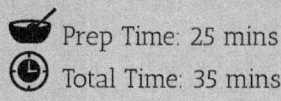 Prep Time: 25 mins
Total Time: 35 mins

Servings per Recipe: 18
Calories   716.1
Fat   57.3g
Cholesterol   32.5mg
Sodium   178.6mg
Carbohydrates   46.7g
Protein   5.3g

Ingredients

2 (1/4 oz.) envelope active dry yeast
1/4 C. warm water
1 1/2 C. lukewarm milk
1/2 C. white sugar
1 tsp salt
2 eggs
1/3 C. shortening

5 C. all-purpose flour
1 quart vegetable oil
Coating
1/3 C. butter
2 C. confectioners' sugar
1 1/2 tsp vanilla
4 tbsp hot water

Directions

1. In a bowl, add the warm water and sprinkle with the yeast.
2. Keep aside for about 5 minutes.
3. In another bowl, add 2 C. of the flour, yeast mixture, milk, eggs, shortening, sugar and salt with an electric mixer, beat on low speed until well combined.
4. Add the remaining flour, 1/2 C. at a time and mix until a non-sticky dough forms.
5. Now, with your hands, knead the dough until smooth and elastic.
6. In a greased bowl, place the dough.
7. With a plastic sheet, cover the dough and keep in a warm area until doubled in bulk.
8. Place the dough onto a floured surface and roll into 1/2-inch thickness.
9. With a floured doughnut cutter, cut the doughnuts.
10. In a deep skillet, add the oil and cook until heated through.
11. Add the doughnuts in batches and cook until golden brown from both sides.
12. With a slotted spoon, transfer the doughnuts onto a paper towel-lined plate to drain.
13. For the glaze: in a pot, add the butter over medium heat and cook until melted.
14. Add the confectioners' sugar and vanilla and stir until smooth.
15. Remove from the heat and stir in the hot water until desired consistency is achieved.
16. Coat the warm doughnuts with the glaze and enjoy.

PEANUT BUTTER
Donuts

Prep Time: 20 mins
Total Time: 35 mins

Servings per Recipe: 8
Calories   310.8
Fat   14.2g
Cholesterol   21.8mg
Sodium   209.1mg
Carbohydrates   42.6g
Protein   5.7g

Ingredients
8 oz. refrigerated crescent dinner rolls
Filling
1/2 C. brown sugar
1/2 C. walnuts
2 tbsp butter, softened
1/2 tsp cinnamon
4 tbsp semi-sweet chocolate chips
2 tbsp peanut butter
3 tbsp peanut butter chips

1/2 C. pie filling, mashed
Glaze
1/2 C. powdered sugar
2 1/2 tsp brewed coffee

Directions
1. Set your oven to 350 degrees F before doing anything else and line a baking sheet with a piece of the foil.
2. For the filling: in a bowl, add all the ingredients and mix well.
3. Unroll the dough and then, carefully divide into crescents.
4. Place the filling onto the wide ends of the crescents, leaving about 1-inch edges.
5. Roll each crescent over the filling into a half moon shape.
6. In the bottom of the prepared baking sheet, arrange the, arrange the about 1-inch apart.
7. Cook in the oven for about 15 minutes.
8. Remove from the oven and keep onto the wire rack to cool in the pan for about 10 minutes.
9. Meanwhile, for the frosting: in a bowl, add the powdered sugar and coffee and beat until well combined.
10. Drizzle the warm doughnuts with the frosting and enjoy.

Yellow Donuts

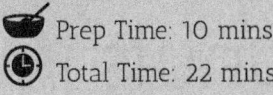 Prep Time: 10 mins
Total Time: 22 mins

Servings per Recipe: 24
Calories   176.4
Fat   7.7g
Cholesterol   23.6mg
Sodium   150.9mg
Carbohydrates   25.5g
Protein   1.7g

Ingredients

1 C. sugar
1 1/2 tsp ground cinnamon
1 (18 1/4 oz.) packages yellow cake mix
1/8 C. water
1/2 C. vegetable oil
3 eggs
1 tbsp ground nutmeg

Directions

1. Set your oven to 350 degrees F before doing anything else and grease 24 cups of a mini muffin pan.
2. In a bowl, add the cinnamon and sugar and mix well.
3. In another bowl, add the cake mix, eggs, oil and water and mix as directed onto the package.
4. Add the nutmeg and stir to combine.
5. In the prepared muffin pan, place the mixture about 2/3 of full.
6. Cook in the oven for about 12 minutes.
7. Coat warm doughnuts with the sugar mixture and enjoy.

SWEET DROPPED
Donuts in Portugal

🥣 Prep Time: 30 mins
🕐 Total Time: 50 mins

Servings per Recipe: 20
Calories 155.5
Fat 4.3g
Cholesterol 129.9mg
Sodium 240.5mg
Carbohydrates 22.0g
Protein 6.3g

Ingredients
1 quart water
1 lemon, zest
1 stick cinnamon
2 tbsp butter
4 C. flour
4 tsp baking powder
4 tbsp sugar
12 eggs

1 tsp salt

Directions
1. In a pan, add the water, lemon rind and cinnamon stick and cook until boiling.
2. Meanwhile, in a bowl, add the flour, sugar, baking powder and salt and mix well.
3. Add the butter into the boiling water and stir until butter is melted completely.
4. Remove from the heat and discard the lemon rind and cinnamon sticks.
5. Place the water into the bowl of the flour mixture and beat vigorously until well combined.
6. Add eggs, 1 at a time and beat well after each addition.
7. In a deep skillet, add the oil and cook until heated through.
8. With a spoon, add the mixture and cook until golden brown from both sides.
9. Add the doughnuts in batches and cook for about 2-4 minutes, flipping once half way through.
10. With a slotted spoon, transfer the doughnuts onto a paper towel-lined plate to drain.
11. Coat the warm doughnuts with the cinnamon sugar and enjoy.

Mexican
Donut Holes
(Bunuelos)

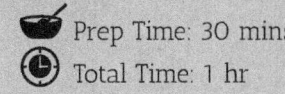 Prep Time: 30 mins

Total Time: 1 hr

Servings per Recipe: 30
Calories	641.5
Fat	19.9g
Cholesterol	167.5mg
Sodium	1211.6mg
Carbohydrates	102.9g
Protein	12.5g

Ingredients

2/3 C. sugar, divided
1 tsp ground cinnamon
1/4 C. butter, softened
2 eggs
1 tsp vanilla extract
1 3/4 C. all-purpose flour, divided
2 tsp baking powder

1 tsp salt
1/4 C. milk
vegetable oil

Directions

1. In a bowl, add the cinnamon and 1/3 C. of the sugar and mix well.
2. Keep aside.
3. In another bowl, add remaining 1/3 C. of the sugar and butter and with an electric mixer; beat until creamy.
4. Add the eggs and vanilla and mix well.
5. Add 1 C. of the flour, baking powder and salt and mix well
6. Add the flour mixture into the bowl of the milk mixture and mix well
7. Add the remaining flour and mix until a soft dough forms.
8. Place onto a floured surface and with your hands, knead for about 2 minutes.
9. With a lightly floured rolling pin, roll the dough into 1/4-inch thickness.
10. Place the dough onto a floured surface and roll into 1/4-inch thickness.
11. With a 2-inch round cookie cutter, cut the doughnuts.
12. In a deep skillet, add 2-inch of the oil over medium heat and cook until heated through.
13. Add the doughnuts in batches and cook for about 3-4 minutes, flipping once half way through.
14. With a slotted spoon, transfer the doughnuts onto a paper towel-lined plate to drain.
15. Coat the warm doughnuts with the cinnamon sugar and enjoy.

DONUTS
in Oslo

Prep Time: 24 h
Total Time: 24 h 10 mins

Servings per Recipe: 10

Calories	322.7
Fat	13.0g
Cholesterol	91.6mg
Sodium	278.6mg
Carbohydrates	45.4g
Protein	6.4g

Ingredients
3 eggs
3/4 C. sugar
2/3 C. whipping cream
2/3 C. sour cream
3 C. flour
2 tbsp baking powder
1 tsp cardamom
2 tbsp butter, melted

Directions
1. In a bowl, add the flour, baking powder and cardamom and mix well.
2. Now, sift the flour mixture into another bowl.
3. In a second bowl, add the sour cream and whipping cream and beat until whipped.
4. In a third bowl, add the sugar and eggs and beat until light and fluffy.
5. Add the flour mixture, alternating with the cream mixture and gently, stir to combine.
6. Refrigerate overnight.
7. Place the dough onto a floured surface and roll into 1-inch thickness.
8. With a doughnut cutter, cut the doughnuts.
9. In a deep skillet, add the oil and cook until its temperature reaches to 350 degrees F.
10. Add the doughnuts in batches and cook until golden brown from both sides.
11. With a slotted spoon, transfer the doughnuts onto a paper towel-lined plate to drain.
12. Enjoy warm.

Cardamom Donuts

🥣 Prep Time: 20 mins
🕐 Total Time: 50 mins

Servings per Recipe: 15
Calories	466.7
Fat	12.3g
Cholesterol	139.9mg
Sodium	172.1mg
Carbohydrates	77.9g
Protein	10.4g

Ingredients

8 eggs
2 C. sugar
8 C. flour
1/2 C. butter, melted
1/2 C. whipping cream
1/8 tsp baking powder
1 tsp baking soda

juice & zest of one lemon
2 tbsp apple juice, optional
sugar
cardamom
oil

Directions

1. In a bowl, add the eggs and beat until lemon colored.
2. Add the flour, sugar, baking soda, baking powder, whipping cream, butter, apple juice, lemon juice and zest and mix until a stiff dough forms.
3. Keep the dough aside overnight.
4. Place the dough onto a floured surface and roll into 1/4-inch thickness.
5. With a doughnut cutter, cut the doughnuts.
6. In a deep skillet, add the oil over medium-high heat and cook until heated through.
7. In a deep skillet, add the oil and cook until its temperature reaches to 350 degrees F.
8. Add the doughnuts in batches and cook until golden brown from both sides.
9. With a slotted spoon, transfer the doughnuts onto a paper towel-lined plate to drain.
10. In a bowl, mix together the sugar and cardamom.
11. Coat the warm doughnuts with the sugar mixture and enjoy.

FRIENDSHIP
Donuts

Prep Time: 30 mins
Total Time: 30 mins

Servings per Recipe: 1
Calories	143.2
Fat	3.5g
Cholesterol	20.3mg
Sodium	395.0mg
Carbohydrates	24.5g
Protein	3.1g

Ingredients

3 eggs
6 C. flour
2 C. warm water
2 tbsp salt
4 tbsp yeast
1/2 C. sugar
1/2 C. lard
Coating

2 tsp white Karo
1 tsp vanilla
1 1/2 C. powdered sugar
2 - 3 tbsp hot water

Directions

1. In a large bowl, add 2 C. of the warm water and yeast and mix until well combined.
2. Add the flour, eggs, lard, sugar and salt and mix until well combined.
3. With a tea towel, cover the dough and keep aside in warm place until doubled in bulk.
4. Place the dough onto a floured surface and roll into 1/2-inch thickness.
5. With a doughnut cutter, cut the doughnuts.
6. With a tea towel, cover the dough and keep aside in warm place for about 30-45 minutes.
7. In a deep skillet, add the oil and cook until heated through.
8. Add the doughnuts in batches and cook until golden brown from both sides.
9. With a slotted spoon, transfer the doughnuts onto a paper towel-lined plate to drain.
10. Meanwhile, for the glaze: in a bowl, add the powdered sugar, Karo syrup, vanilla, and 2 tbsp of the hot water and mix until well combined.
11. Coat the warm doughnuts with the glaze and enjoy.

Candy
Donuts

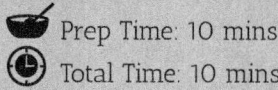 Prep Time: 10 mins

Total Time: 10 mins

Servings per Recipe: 8	
Calories	2457.4
Fat	253.0g
Cholesterol	0.5mg
Sodium	568.0mg
Carbohydrates	52.7g
Protein	3.9g

Ingredients

1 (16 oz.) cans Pillsbury Grands
refrigerated buttermilk biscuits
9 C. oil
1 C. sugar
1/4 C. cinnamon
1 (16 oz.) cans icing
candy sprinkles

Directions

1. With the cap of a bottle, cut a hole in the center of each biscuits.
2. In a deep skillet, add the oil and cook until its temperature reaches to 375 degrees F.
3. Add the doughnuts in batches and cook, covered for about 6 minutes, flipping once half way through.
4. With a slotted spoon, transfer the doughnuts onto a paper towel-lined plate to drain.
5. Meanwhile, in a bowl, add the cinnamon and sugar and mix well.
6. Coat the warm doughnuts with the cinnamon sugar, icing and sprinkles and enjoy.

ALL-PURPOSE
Donut

Prep Time: 20 mins
Total Time: 2 hr 20 mins

Servings per Recipe: 20
Calories	184.7
Fat	5.1g
Cholesterol	23.7mg
Sodium	191.8mg
Carbohydrates	29.0g
Protein	5.2g

Ingredients
1 1/2 C. milk
2 1/2 oz. vegetable shortening
2 1/2 tbsp instant yeast
1/3 C. warm water
2 eggs, beaten
1/4 C. sugar
1 1/2 tsp salt
1 tsp nutmeg
23 oz. all-purpose flour
peanut oil

Directions
1. In a pot, add the milk over medium heat and cook until just warmed.
2. In a bowl, add the shortening and top with the warm milk.
3. Keep aside.
4. In another bowl, add the warm water and sprinkle with the yeast.
5. Keep aside for about 5 minutes.
6. In the bowl of a stand mixer, attached with the paddle attachment, add the yeast mixture, eggs, lukewarm milk mixture, sugar, half of the flour, nutmeg and salt and beat on low speed until combined.
7. Now, increase the speed to medium and beat until well combined.
8. Add the remaining flour and mix on low speed.
9. Now, increase the speed to medium and beat until well combined.
10. Now, set the mixer to the dough hook attachment and beat on medium speed until a smooth dough forms.
11. Place the dough into a generously greased bowl.
12. Cover the bowl and keep aside in warm place for about 1 hour.

13. Place the dough onto a generously floured surface and roll into 3/8-inch thickness.
14. With a 2 1/2-inch doughnut cutter, cut the doughnuts.
15. Then, with the cap of a bottle, cut a hole in the center of each doughnut.
16. In the bottom of a floured baking sheet, arrange the doughnuts.
17. With a tea towel, cover the baking sheet lightly and keep aside for about 30 minutes.
18. In a deep skillet, add the oil and cook until its temperature reaches to 375 degrees F.
19. Add the doughnuts in batches and cook for about 2 minutes, flipping once half way through.
20. With a slotted spoon, transfer the doughnuts onto a paper towel-lined plate to drain.
21. Keep aside to cool for about 15-20 minutes.
22. Enjoy.

HOW TO MAKE
Donut Glaze

Prep Time: 5 mins
Total Time: 7 mins

Servings per Recipe: 1
Calories   39.7
Fat   0.0g
Cholesterol   0.2mg
Sodium   1.1mg
Carbohydrates   9.7g
Protein   0.0g

Ingredients
1/4 C. whole milk
1 tsp almond extract
1 tsp vanilla extract
2 C. confectioners' sugar, sifted

Directions
1. In a pan, add the milk and vanilla over low heat and cook until warm.
2. Add the sifted confectioners' sugar and beat until well combined.
3. Remove the glaze from the heat and arrange over a bowl of the warm water.
4. coat your doughnuts with the glaze and enjoy

Caribbean
Cocoa Donuts

Prep Time: 40 mins
Total Time: 1 hr 10 mins

Servings per Recipe: 12
Calories	272.6
Fat	5.5g
Cholesterol	38.1mg
Sodium	240.3mg
Carbohydrates	49.2g
Protein	6.2g

Ingredients

3 tbsp cooking oil
1 C. granulated sugar
2 eggs
1 C. milk
1 tsp vanilla
3 3/4 C. all-purpose flour
4 tsp baking powder

1/2 tsp salt
1/3 C. cocoa

Directions

1. In a bowl, add 3 tbsp of the oil, milk, eggs, sugar and vanilla and mix well.
2. Add the flour, cocoa powder, baking powder and salt and mix until well combined.
3. With a doughnut cutter, cut the doughnuts.
4. Then, with the cap of a bottle, cut a hole in the center of each doughnut.
5. In a deep skillet, add the oil and cook until its temperature reaches to 375 degrees F.
6. Add the doughnuts in batches and cook until golden brown from both sides.
7. Add the doughnuts in batches and cook for about 2-4 minutes, flipping once half way through.
8. With a slotted spoon, transfer the doughnuts onto a paper towel-lined plate to drain.
9. Enjoy.

LEMON
Donuts

Prep Time: 30 mins
Total Time: 1 hr 10 mins

Servings per Recipe: 1
Calories	71.6
Fat	1.6g
Cholesterol	17.9mg
Sodium	34.6mg
Carbohydrates	12.7g
Protein	1.4g

Ingredients

3/4 C. butter
3 C. sugar
8 eggs, beaten
2 lemons, zest
1 tsp lemon flavoring
9 - 9 1/2 C. all-purpose flour, divided
1/2 tsp salt
1 tsp baking soda

2 tsp cream of tartar
oil

Directions

1. In a bowl, add 4 C. of the flour, baking soda, cream of tartar and salt and mix well.
2. In another bowl, add the sugar and butter and beat until creamy.
3. Add the eggs, lemon flavoring and lemon zest and mix well.
4. Add the flour mixture and mix until well combined.
5. Add the remaining flour, 1 C. at a time and mix until a very stiff dough forms.
6. With your hand, roll the dough into 1-inch-thick snake like rolls.
7. Then, cut each roll into 2-inch long fingers.
8. Place in the fridge for whole night.
9. In a deep skillet, add the oil and cook until heated through.
10. Add the dough fingers in batches and cook until golden brown from both sides.
11. Add the doughnuts in batches and cook for about 2-4 minutes, flipping once half way through.
12. Enjoy.

Clove
Donuts

Prep Time: 15 mins
Total Time: 35 mins

Servings per Recipe: 12
Calories   95.5
Fat   1.1g
Cholesterol   0.8mg
Sodium   49.4mg
Carbohydrates   17.9g
Protein   3.7g

Ingredients

6 egg whites
1 C. buttermilk
2 tsp safflower oil
1/2 C. whole wheat flour
1/2 C. all-purpose flour
2/3 C. powdered sugar
1/4 tsp nutmeg, ground

1/4 tsp clove, ground
1/8 tsp mace
1/4 tsp cinnamon
1/4 C. powdered sugar

Directions

1. Set your oven to 400 degrees F before doing anything else and lightly grease cups of a muffin pan.
2. In a bowl, add the egg whites and beat until frothy.
3. Add the oil and buttermilk and beat until well combined.
4. Add the flours, powdered sugar, mace, nutmeg, cinnamon and cloves and beat until smooth.
5. In the prepared muffin cups, place the mixture evenly.
6. Cook in the oven for about 20 minutes.
7. Remove from the oven and place the pan onto a wire rack for about 1 minute.
8. Carefully, remove the doughnuts from the pan and keep aside to cool for about 4-5 minutes.
9. Enjoy with a dusting of the powdered sugar.

APPLE RAISIN
Donuts

Prep Time: 2 hr
Total Time: 2 hr 5 mins

Servings per Recipe: 20
Calories	100.9
Fat	0.9g
Cholesterol	11.0mg
Sodium	243.8mg
Carbohydrates	21.3g
Protein	2.6g

Ingredients
7 g dry yeast
1 C. light blue capped milk
2 1/4 C. flour
2 tsp salt
1 egg, beaten
1 1/2 C. raisins
1 apple, peeled, cored and chopped
oil

powdered sugar

Directions
1. In a bowl, place 1/4 C. of the milk and sprinkle with the yeast.
2. Keep aide for about 5 minutes.
3. In another bowl, add the flour and salt and mix well.
4. Add the egg and remaining milk and beat until well combined.
5. Add the yeast mixture, apple and raisins and mix until well combined.
6. Keep aside in a warm area until doubled in bulk.
7. With 2 metal spoons, make the balls from the mixture.
8. In a deep skillet, add the oil and cook until its temperature reaches to 325 degrees F.
9. Add the doughnuts in batches and cook for about 8 minutes, flipping frequently.
10. With a slotted spoon, transfer the doughnuts onto a paper towel-lined plate to drain.
11. Coat the doughnuts with the powdered sugar and keep aside to cool.
12. After cooling, coat with the powdered sugar and enjoy.

Sweet
Dinner Roll Donuts

Prep Time: 20 mins
Total Time: 30 mins

Servings per Recipe: 4
Calories	1259.2
Fat	113.7g
Cholesterol	29.0mg
Sodium	483.2mg
Carbohydrates	57.7g
Protein	5.9g

Ingredients

2 C. vegetable oil
1 (8 oz.) cans Pillsbury Refrigerated
Crescent Dinner Rolls
1 snack-size container vanilla pudding
2 tbsp caramel sauce

1/4 tsp kosher salt
1/2 C. powdered sugar
milk
additional caramel sauce

Directions

1. Separate the crescent dough into 4 rectangles and press the holes tightly to seal.
2. arrange 2 rectangles onto a smooth surface.
3. Top each with another rectangle.
4. Now, fold each stack in half widthwise.
5. With a 3-inch biscuit cutter, cut 1 round from each stack and then, with a 1/2-inch biscuit cutter, cut a small hole in center of each round.
6. Reroll the remaining dough from both stacks and make a third doughnut in the same way.
7. In a deep skillet, add the oil and cook until its temperature reaches to 325 degrees F.
8. Add the doughnuts in batches and cook until golden brown from both sides.
9. Add the doughnuts and cook for about 5 minutes, flipping once half way through.
10. With a slotted spoon, transfer the doughnuts onto a paper towel-lined plate to drain.
11. Keep aside to cool for about 5 minutes.
12. Carefully, cut each doughnut in half.
13. In a pipping bag, fitted with tip, place the pudding.
14. Pipe half of the pudding onto the bottom half of each doughnut and top each with some of the caramel sauce and salt.
15. Cover each bottom half with the top of doughnut.
16. For the glaze: in a bowl, add the powdered sugar and enough milk and mix until a desired consistency is achieved.
17. Coat the top of each doughnut with the laze.
18. Enjoy with a drizzling of the caramel sauce.

ONTARIO
Donut Squares

Prep Time: 1 hr
Total Time: 1 hr 3 mins

Servings per Recipe: 1

Calories	7186.2
Fat	193.5g
Cholesterol	600.7mg
Sodium	4600.1mg
Carbohydrates	1238.6g
Protein	117.8g

Ingredients
2 tbsp yeast
1/2 C. warm water
6 tbsp margarine
1 C. milk, scalding
1 C. cold water
1 tsp salt
1/2 C. sugar
3 eggs

6 -7 C. flour
oil
Glaze
4 1/2 C. powdered sugar
1/2 C. margarine
4 tbsp milk
2 tbsp maple flavoring

Directions
1. In a bowl, add 1/2 of the water and sprinkle with the yeast.
2. Keep aside for about 5 minutes.
3. In another bowl, add the hot scalded milk, butter, sugar and salt and sugar and stir well.
4. Add the cold water and mix until well combined.
5. In the bowl of the mixer, add the yeast mixture and milk mixture.
6. Add flour, 1 C. at a time and mix until a soft dough forms.
7. Place the dough onto a lightly floured surface and with a rolling pin, roll into a 1/4-1/2 inch thick rectangle.
8. Cut the dough into 2-3x5-6-inch rectangular bars.
9. With a plastic wrap, over the bars and keep aside until doubled in size.
10. In a deep skillet, add the oil and cook until its temperature reaches to 350 degrees F.
11. Add the doughnut bars in batches and cook until golden brown from both sides.
12. With a slotted spoon, transfer the doughnuts onto a paper towel-lined plate to drain.
13. Meanwhile, for the frosting: in a bowl, add all the ingredients and beat until smooth.
14. Coat the doughnuts with the frosting and enjoy.

Doughnuts
Toscano

Prep Time: 2 hr
Total Time: 2 hr 2 mins

Servings per Recipe: 1
Calories   193.3
Fat   2.6g
Cholesterol   0.0mg
Sodium   226.3mg
Carbohydrates   38.9g
Protein   3.5g

Ingredients

Dough
1 1/3 C. water
3 tsp sugar
1 tsp salt
2 tbsp olive oil
2 tbsp cornmeal
3 C. unbleached all-purpose flour
1 tsp baking powder

1 1/2 tsp bread machine yeast
Donut
vegetable oil
olive oil
1 lb. prepared pizza dough
3/4 C. sugar
1 1/2 tsp ground cinnamon

Directions

1. In the pan of bread machine, place the dough ingredients in order as suggested by the manual.
2. Select the Dough cycle and press the Start button.
3. Place the dough onto a floured surface and roll into 1/2-inch thickness.
4. With a floured 2-inch cookie cutter, cut the doughnuts.
5. Then, with the cap of a bottle, cut a hole in the center of each doughnut.
6. In a deep skillet, add the same quantity of both oils over medium heat and cook until its temperature reaches to 375 degrees F.
7. Add the doughnuts in batches and cook until golden brown from both sides.
8. Add the doughnuts in batches and cook for about 1 1/2 minutes, flipping once half way through.
9. With a slotted spoon, transfer the doughnuts onto a paper towel-lined plate to drain.
10. Meanwhile, in a bowl, add the cinnamon and sugar and mix well.
11. Coat the warm doughnuts with the cinnamon sugar and enjoy.

DONUTS
Rhode Island

Prep Time: 20 mins
Total Time: 40 mins

Servings per Recipe: 1

Calories	1225.3
Fat	33.7g
Cholesterol	105.8mg
Sodium	1250.4mg
Carbohydrates	197.8g
Protein	30.1g

Ingredients
1 (1/4 oz.) package dry active yeast
1/4 C. warm water
3/4 C. warm milk
1/4 C. sugar
1 tsp salt
1 egg
1/4 C. shortening
3 1/2-3 3/4 C. all-purpose flour

Directions
1. In a bowl, add the warm water and yeast and mix until well combined.
2. Add the shortening, milk, egg, 2 C. of the flour, sugar and salt and mix until well combined.
3. Add the remaining flour and mix until a dough forms.
4. Place the dough onto a lightly floured surface and with your hands, knead until smooth and elastic.
5. In a lightly greased bowl, place the dough and turn to coat evenly.
6. With a damp cloth, cover the bowl and keep aside in warm area for about 1 1/2 hours.
7. With your hands, punch down the dough and With a damp cloth, cover the bowl and keep aside in warm area for about 30 minute.
8. Place the dough onto a floured surface and roll into 3/8-inch thickness.
9. With a doughnut cutter, cut the doughnuts.
10. Keep aside in for about 30 minute.
11. In a deep skillet, add the oil and cook until its temperature reaches to 375 degrees F.
12. Add the doughnuts in batches and cook until golden brown from both sides.
13. With a slotted spoon, transfer the doughnuts onto a paper towel-lined plate to drain.
14. Enjoy warm.

Donuts Rhode Island

Sweet
Carrot Donuts
(Gluten Free)

🥣 Prep Time: 30 mins
🕐 Total Time: 38 mins

Servings per Recipe: 12
Calories   118.2
Fat   5.7g
Cholesterol   0.0mg
Sodium   81.7mg
Carbohydrates   15.9g
Protein   1.5g

Ingredients

1 1/2 tbsp ground flax seeds
1/4 C. hot water
1/3 C. brown rice flour
1/4 C. chickpea flour
1/4 C. arrowroot
1/2 tsp guar gum
3/4 tsp baking powder
1/2 tsp cinnamon
1/4 tsp nutmeg
1/4 tsp ginger
1/4 tsp salt
2 tbsp ground pecans
3 tbsp cream of rice
2 tbsp fine cornmeal
1/3 C. unsweetened vanilla almond milk
3 tbsp brown sugar
2 tbsp maple syrup
1 tbsp oil
1/2 tbsp vanilla
2/3 C. grated carrot
1/4 C. medium-shredded unsweetened coconut

Directions

1. Set your oven to 425 degrees F before doing anything else and lightly, grease a doughnut pan.
2. In a bowl, add the hot water and flax and mix well.
3. Keep aside.
4. In a second bowl, add the cornstarch, flours, brown rice cereal, pecans, guar gum, baking powder, cinnamon, ginger, nutmeg and salt and mix well.
5. In a third bowl, add the maple syrup, almond milk, oil, brown sugar and vanilla and beat until well combined.
6. Add the flax mixture and beat until well combined.
7. Add the flour mixture and mix until well combined.
8. Gently, fold in the coconut and carrots.
9. In the prepared doughnut holes, place the mixture evenly.
10. Cook in the oven for about 8 minutes.
11. Remove from the oven and place onto a wire rack to cool for about 5 minutes.
12. Carefully, remove the doughnuts from the pan and enjoy.

GLAZED HARVEST
Donuts

Prep Time: 10 mins
Total Time: 20 mins

Servings per Recipe: 12
Calories	96.9
Fat	4.5g
Cholesterol	26.9mg
Sodium	148.0mg
Carbohydrates	12.2g
Protein	2.7g

Ingredients
1 1/4 oz. yeast, package
1/4 C. warm water
1/2 C. of lukewarm milk
1/4 C. lukewarm buttermilk
1/2 tsp salt
3 tbsp melted butter
1/4 C. sugar
2 1/2 C. gluten-free flour
1 egg

4 drops of essential lemon oil, optional
4 drops of essential lavender oil, optional
3/4 C. of lukewarm milk
Glaze
1/2 C. powdered sugar
3 tbsp blueberries
1/2 tsp vanilla
1 - 2 tsp milk

Directions
1. Set your oven to 425 degrees F before doing anything else and lightly, grease a doughnut pan.
2. In a bowl, add the warm water and yeast and mix well.
3. Add the butter, buttermilk, 1/2 C. of the milk, eggs, flour, sugar and salt and beat until well combined.
4. With a plastic wrap, cover the bowl and keep aside for about 50-60 minutes.
5. Add 3/4 C. of the milk and mix until a dough forms.
6. In the prepared doughnut holes, place the mixture evenly.
7. Cook in the oven for about 7-10 minutes.
8. Meanwhile, for the glaze: in a food processor, add all the ingredients and pulse until smooth.
9. Carefully, remove the doughnuts from the pan and keep aside to cool.
10. Coat the cooled doughnuts with the glaze and enjoy.

Vanilla
Rice Milk Donuts

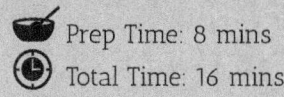 Prep Time: 8 mins

Total Time: 16 mins

Servings per Recipe: 1
Calories	82.0
Fat	1.1g
Cholesterol	0.0mg
Sodium	41.5mg
Carbohydrates	16.3g
Protein	1.4g

Ingredients

2 C. flour
1/2 C. vegan sugar
2 tsp baking powder
1 1/2 tsp egg substitute
2 tbsp water
3/4 C. rice milk
1 tsp vanilla extract

4 tsp cooking oil
cinnamon sugar

Directions

1. Set your oven to 325 degrees F before doing anything else and lightly, grease a doughnut pan.
2. In a mug, add the egg substitute and water and mix well.
3. In a bowl, add the flour, baking powder and sugar and mix well.
4. Add the oil, rice milk, egg substitute mixture and vanilla and beat until well combined.
5. In the prepared doughnut holes, place the mixture evenly.
6. Cook in the oven for about 8-10 minutes.
7. Carefully, remove the doughnuts from the pan.
8. Coat with the cinnamon sugar and enjoy.

NEW HAMPSHIRE
Donuts

Prep Time: 20 mins
Total Time: 50 mins

Servings per Recipe: 24
Calories	124.8
Fat	2.3g
Cholesterol	28.6mg
Sodium	142.3mg
Carbohydrates	22.8g
Protein	2.8g

Ingredients
1 C. sour milk
4 egg yolks
2 tbsp melted shortening
1/2 tsp vanilla
4 C. flour
1 tsp salt
1/2 tsp cream of tartar
3/4 C. sugar

1/2 tsp nutmeg
1 tsp cinnamon
3/4 tsp baking soda
oil

Directions
1. In a bowl, add the flour, baking soda, cinnamon, nutmeg and salt and mix well.
2. Now, sift the flour mixture into a second bowl.
3. In another bowl, add the egg yolks and beat until lemon colored.
4. Add the sugar and beat until well combined.
5. Add the shortening, milk, cream of tartar and vanilla and beat until well combined.
6. Add the flour mixture and mix until a sticky dough forms.
7. Place the dough onto a floured surface and roll into 3/4-inch thickness.
8. With a doughnut cutter, cut the doughnuts.
9. In a deep skillet, add the oil and cook until its temperature reaches to 350 degrees F.
10. Add the doughnuts in batches and cook until golden brown from both sides.
11. With a slotted spoon, transfer the doughnuts onto a paper towel-lined plate to drain.
12. Coat the warm doughnuts with the powdered sugar and enjoy.

Seattle
Chocolate Donuts (Vegan)

Prep Time: 1 hr
Total Time: 1 hr 30 mins

Servings per Recipe: 30
Calories   77.5
Fat   2.3g
Cholesterol   0.0mg
Sodium   122.7mg
Carbohydrates   12.8g
Protein   2.3g

Ingredients

1 1/2 C. granulated beet sugar
3 tsp Ener-G Egg Substitute, mixed with 4 tbsp water
4 tbsp non-hydrogenated vegan margarine
4 oz. unsweetened baking chocolate

1 1/2 tsp pure vanilla extract
1 C. soy milk, mixed with 1 tsp white vinegar
3 1/2 C. unbleached flour
3 tsp baking powder
1 tsp baking soda
1/2 tsp salt

Directions

1. In a bowl, add the sugar and the egg replacer and beat until creamy.
2. In a pan, add the chocolate and margarine over low heat and cook until melted completely, stirring continuously.
3. Remove from the heat and keep aside to cool.
4. Add the chocolate mixture into the sugar mixture and beat until well combined.
5. In another bowl, add the vinegar, soy milk and vanilla and mix well.
6. Add the vinegar mixture into the chocolate mixture and mix well.
7. In a third bowl, add the flour, baking soda, baking powder and salt and mix well.
8. Add the flour mixture into the chocolate mixture and mix until a dough forms.
9. Refrigerate for about 30 minutes.
10. Place the dough onto a floured surface and roll into 1/2-inch thickness.
11. With a doughnut cutter, cut the doughnuts.
12. Keep aside for about 10 minutes.
13. In a deep skillet, add the oil and cook until heated through.
14. Add the doughnuts in batches and cook for about 90 seconds, flipping after every 15 seconds.
15. With a slotted spoon, transfer the doughnuts onto a paper towel-lined plate to drain.
16. Coat the warm doughnuts with the powdered sugar and enjoy.

WHITE BREAD
Mock "Donuts"

Prep Time: 15 mins
Total Time: 30 mins

Servings per Recipe: 1

Calories	68.7
Fat	1.8g
Cholesterol	31.7mg
Sodium	131.5mg
Carbohydrates	10.0g
Protein	2.7g

Ingredients
24 slices white bread, crusts removed
5 eggs
2 1/2 C. milk
2 tbsp sugar
2 tsp vanilla extract
jam
icing sugar

Directions
1. In a bowl, add the milk, eggs, sugar and Vanilla and beat until well combined.
2. Place the jam onto 12 bread slices evenly and top each with 1 of the remaining slices.
3. Then cut each sandwich into 3-4 pieces.
4. Coat each doughnut piece with the egg mixture evenly.
5. In a deep skillet, add the oil and cook until its temperature reaches to 375 degrees F.
6. Add the doughnuts in batches and cook for about 4 minutes, flipping once half way through.
7. With a slotted spoon, transfer the doughnuts onto a paper towel-lined plate to drain.
8. Coat the warm doughnuts with the icing sugar and enjoy.

Cobb County Donuts

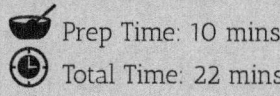 Prep Time: 10 mins

Total Time: 22 mins

Servings per Recipe: 24

Calories	163.1
Fat	8.1g
Cholesterol	28.2mg
Sodium	154.3mg
Carbohydrates	21.2g
Protein	1.8g

Ingredients

2 1/4 C. flour
1 tbsp baking powder
1 tsp baking soda
1 pinch salt
1/4 tsp nutmeg
4 tbsp brown sugar
1 C. sour cream
1 egg

1/4 C. melted butter
1 tsp vanilla
1/2 C. frozen blueberries
Coating
1 C. white sugar
1/2 tbsp cinnamon
1/2-1 C. melted butter

Directions

1. Set your oven to 400 degrees F before doing anything else and grease 24 cups of a mini muffin pan.
2. In a bowl, add the flour, brown sugar, baking powder, baking soda, nutmeg and salt and mix well.
3. In another bowl, add the sour cream, butter and vanilla and beat until well combined.
4. Add the blueberries and stir to combine.
5. Add the flour mixture and mix until just combined.
6. In the prepared muffin pan, place the mixture evenly.
7. Cook in the oven for about 12-15 minutes.
8. Remove from the oven and keep onto a wire rack to cool for about 2 minutes.
9. Carefully, remove the doughnuts from the pan and keep onto a wire rack to cool for about 5 minutes.
10. Meanwhile, in a bowl, add the cinnamon and sugar and mix well.
11. Coat the doughnuts with the butter and then with cinnamon sugar.
12. Enjoy.

5 MINUTE
Hazelnut Topped Donut

Prep Time: 5 mins
Total Time: 5 mins

Servings per Recipe: 1

Calories	441.9
Fat	24.6g
Cholesterol	3.6mg
Sodium	220.3mg
Carbohydrates	49.5g
Protein	5.8g

Ingredients
1 doughnut, glazed, halved horizontally
2 tbsp Nutella chocolate hazelnut spread

Directions
1. Place the Nutella onto both cut sides of doughnut halves.
2. Place the top half onto bottom half and enjoy.
3. Enjoy.

Hawaiian
Drop Donuts

Prep Time: 15 mins
Total Time: 40 mins

Servings per Recipe: 18
Calories   148.6
Fat   1.5g
Cholesterol   37.1mg
Sodium   236.9mg
Carbohydrates   30.2g
Protein   3.7g

Ingredients

3 C. all-purpose flour
3/4 C. sugar
2 tbsp baking powder
3/4 tsp salt
3 eggs, beaten
1 C. milk
1 (20 oz.) cans crushed pineapple, drained
vegetable oil
powdered sugar

Directions

1. In a bowl, add the flour, baking powder, sugar and salt and mix until blended.
2. Add the eggs, milk and pineapple and mix until smooth.
3. In a deep skillet, add 3-4-inch of the oil and cook until its temperature reaches to 375 degrees F.
4. With a tbsp, add the mixture in batches and cook for about 2 minutes, flipping once half way through.
5. With a slotted spoon, transfer the doughnuts onto a paper towel-lined plate to drain.
6. Coat the warm doughnuts with the powdered sugar and enjoy.

OCTOBER
Yam Donuts

Prep Time: 15 mins
Total Time: 35 mins

Servings per Recipe: 20

Calories	163.1
Fat	3.1g
Cholesterol	26.2mg
Sodium	143.8mg
Carbohydrates	30.2g
Protein	3.4g

Ingredients

3 1/2 C. flour
1 C. sugar
2 tsp baking powder
1/2 tsp baking soda
1/2 tsp ground cinnamon
1/2 tsp salt
2 large eggs, beaten
1 C. sour cream

1 C. cooked mashed sweet potato
vegetable oil

Directions

1. In a bowl, add the flour, baking soda, baking powder, sugar, cinnamon and salt and mix well.
2. In another bowl, add the sour cream, eggs and sweet potato and beat until well combined.
3. Add the flour mixture and mix until well combined.
4. Place the dough onto a generously floured surface and with your hands, knead until a sticky dough forms.
5. Now, roll the dough into 1/2-inch thickness.
6. With a 2 1/4-inch doughnut cutter, cut the doughnuts.
7. In a deep skillet, add the oil and cook until its temperature reaches to 360 degrees F.
8. Add the doughnuts in batches and cook for about 2 minutes, flipping once half way through.
9. With a slotted spoon, transfer the doughnuts onto a paper towel-lined plate to drain.
10. Enjoy warm.

White Donuts

Prep Time: 2 hr
Total Time: 2 hr 15 mins

Servings per Recipe: 12
Calories   364.1
Fat   19.1g
Cholesterol   42.4mg
Sodium   147.4mg
Carbohydrates   45.3g
Protein   7.4g

Ingredients
3 1/4 C. flour
2 tsp baking powder
1/4 tsp salt
2 beaten eggs
2/3 C. sugar
2 oz. melted white chocolate
2 tbsp melted butter

1/2 C. milk
1 tsp vanilla
1 C. chocolate, glaze
1 C. chopped macadamia nuts

Directions
1. In a bowl, add the flour, baking powder and salt and mix well.
2. Now, sift the flour mixture into a second bowl.
3. In another bowl, add the sugar and eggs and beat until creamy.
4. Add the butter and chocolate and mix well.
5. Add the milk and vanilla and mix until well combined.
6. Slowly, add the flour mixture and mix until a soft dough forms.
7. With a plastic wrap, cover the dough and place in the fridge for about 2 hours.
8. Place the dough onto a floured surface and roll into 1/2-inch thickness.
9. With a doughnut cutter, cut the doughnuts.
10. In a deep skillet, add the oil and cook until heated through.
11. Add the doughnuts in batches and cook for about 2 minutes, flipping once half way through.
12. With a slotted spoon, transfer the doughnuts onto a paper towel-lined plate to drain.
13. Coat the warm doughnuts with the chocolate glaze.
14. Enjoy with a sprinkling of the nuts.

HOMEMADE
Crullers

Prep Time: 20 mins
Total Time: 35 mins

Servings per Recipe: 1

Calories	300.9
Fat	21.3g
Cholesterol	18.9mg
Sodium	105.1mg
Carbohydrates	25.2g
Protein	2.8g

Ingredients
1/4 C. shortening
3/4 C. granulated sugar
2 large eggs, separated
1/2 tsp vanilla extract
3 1/2 C. all-purpose flour
3 tsp baking powder
1/2 tsp salt
1/4 tsp ground mace

1/4 tsp ground nutmeg
1 1/4 C. whole milk, homogenized
2 C. cooking oil
Topping
1/2 C. granulated sugar
1 1/2 tsp ground cinnamon

Directions
1. In a bowl, add the flour, baking powder, nutmeg, mace and mix well.
2. In a second bowl, add the sugar and shortening and with an electric mixer, beat until fluffy.
3. In a third bowl, add the egg yolks and beat well.
4. Add the beaten egg yolks into the sugar mixture and beat until well combined.
5. Add the vanilla extract and beat until well combined.
6. Add the flour mixture, alternating with the milk and beat until well combined.
7. In a clean glass bowl, add the egg whites and beat until peaks form.
8. Gently, fold the whipped egg whites into the flour mixture.
9. Place the dough onto a floured surface and roll into 1/2-inch thickness.
10. With a doughnut cutter, cut the doughnuts.
11. In a deep skillet, add the oil and cook until its temperature reaches to 375 degrees F.
12. Add the doughnuts in batches and cook until golden brown from both sides.
13. With a slotted spoon, transfer the doughnuts onto a paper towel-lined plate to drain.
14. Meanwhile, in a bowl, add the cinnamon and sugar and mix well.
15. Coat the warm doughnuts with the cinnamon sugar and enjoy.

Glazed
Expresso Donuts

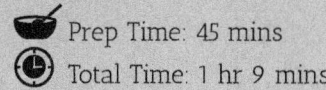 Prep Time: 45 mins

Total Time: 1 hr 9 mins

Servings per Recipe: 1 batch
Calories	22371.2
Fat	2252.1g
Cholesterol	699.7mg
Sodium	4239.2mg
Carbohydrates	551.4g
Protein	61.7g

Ingredients

1 (1/4 oz.) package active dry yeast
2 tbsp warm water
3 1/4 C. all-purpose flour
additional all-purpose flour
1 C. whole milk
1/4 C. unsalted butter, softened
3 large egg yolks
2 tbsp sugar
1 1/2 tsp salt
1/2 tsp cinnamon

10 C. vegetable oil
Glaze
1/4 C. boiling-hot water
5 tsp instant espresso powder
1 1/2 C. confectioners' sugar
1 tbsp light corn syrup
1/4 tsp pure vanilla extract
1/4 tsp salt
1/4 C. sugar

Directions

1. In a bowl, add the warm water and yeast and mix until well combined.
2. Keep aside for about 5 minutes.
3. In the bowl of a mixer, add the yeast mixture, flour, sugar, butter, milk, egg yolks, cinnamon and salt and beat on low speed until a soft dough forms.
4. Now, set the speed to medium-high and beat for about 3 minutes.
5. With a clean kitchen towel, cover the dough and keep aside at warm area for about 1 1/2-2 hours.
6. Place the dough onto a floured surface and roll into 1/2-inch thickness.
7. With a doughnut cutter, cut the doughnuts.
8. In the bottom of a floured baking sheet, arrange the doughnuts.
9. With a clean kitchen towel, cover the baking sheet and keep aside in a warm area for about 30 minutes.
10. In a deep skillet, add 2-inch of the oil and cook until its temperature reaches to 350 degrees F.

11. Add the doughnuts in batches and cook for about 1 minute, flipping once half way through.
12. With a slotted spoon, transfer the doughnuts onto a paper towel-lined plate to drain.
13. Meanwhile, for the glaze: in a bowl, add the espresso powder and boiling water and mix until well combined.
14. Add the corn syrup, vanilla, confectioners' sugar and salt and stir until smooth.
15. Coat the doughnuts with the mixture and place onto a wire rack.
16. Dust the doughnuts with the sanding sugar and keep aside for about 20 minutes.
17. Enjoy.

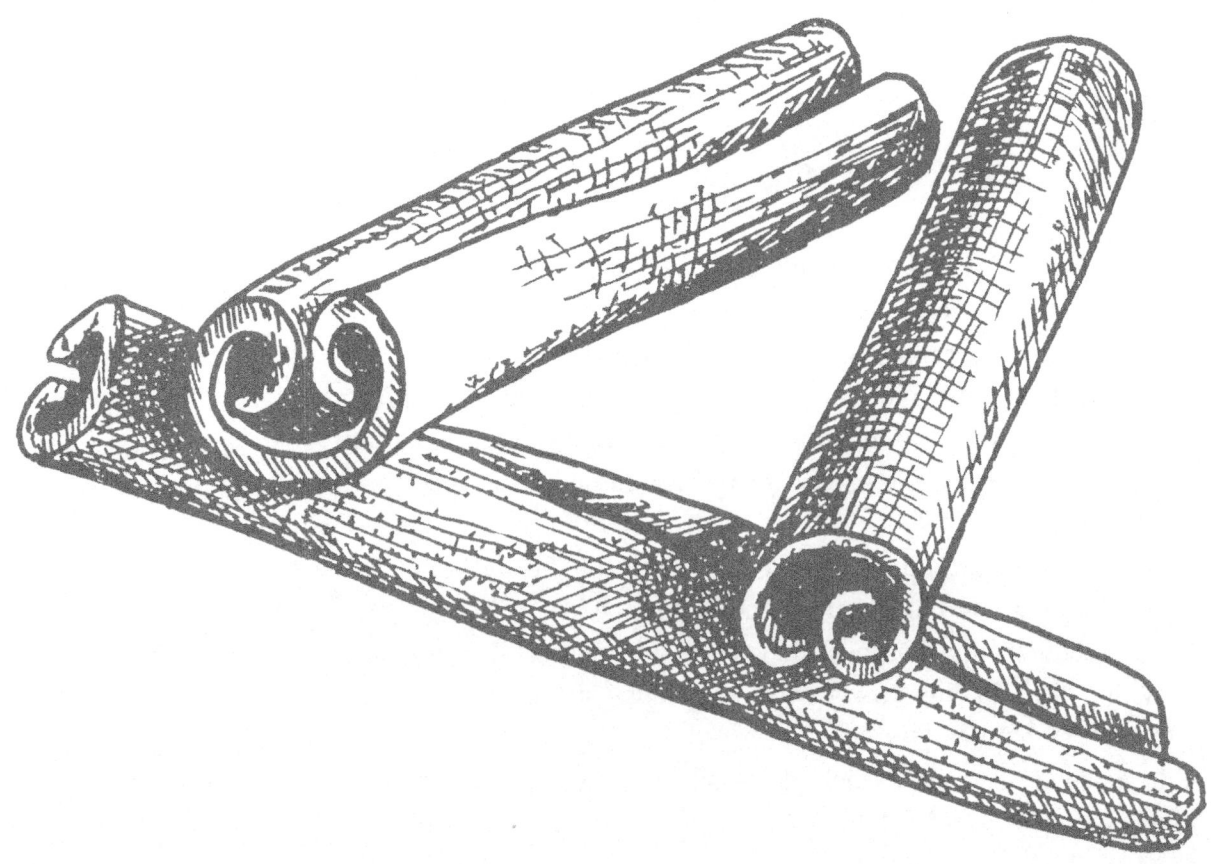

Jelly Doughnuts

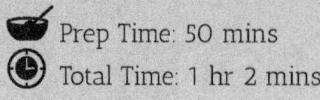 Prep Time: 50 mins

Total Time: 1 hr 2 mins

Servings per Recipe: 20
Calories	145.7
Fat	1.0g
Cholesterol	12.2mg
Sodium	18.0mg
Carbohydrates	29.6g
Protein	4.0g

Ingredients

500 g plain flour
1 pinch salt
50 g caster sugar
7 g instant yeast
1 beaten egg

250 ml lukewarm milk
jam (grape, raspberry, blueberry, etc.)
50 g caster sugar
1/2 tsp ground cinnamon

Directions

1. In a bowl, add the flour and salt and mix well.
2. Now, sift the flour mixture into a second bowl.
3. Add the yeast and 50g sugar and mix well.
4. With your hands, create a well in the center of the flour mixture.
5. In the well, add the milk and beaten egg and mix until a dough forms.
6. Place the dough onto a floured surface and with your hands, knead until a soft dough forms.
7. Make 20 equal sized balls from the mixture.
8. Arrange the dough onto a greased baking sheet.
9. With a damp tea towel, cover the baking sheet and keep aside in a warm area until doubled in size.
10. Set your oven to 425 degree F.
11. Cook in the oven for about 12-15 minutes.
12. Remove from the oven and keep aside to cool slightly.
13. Meanwhile, in a bowl, add the cinnamon and extra sugar and mix well.
14. With your finger, make a small hole in the center of each doughnut.
15. Place 1 tsp of the jam in the hole of each doughnut.
16. Coat with the water lightly.
17. Now, coat with the cinnamon sugar and enjoy.

TROPICAL
Orange Donuts

🥣 Prep Time: 1 hr
🕐 Total Time: 1 hr 50 mins

Servings per Recipe: 1
Calories   366.2
Fat   7.8g
Cholesterol   84.6mg
Sodium   102.4mg
Carbohydrates   68.8g
Protein   6.4g

Ingredients
4 eggs
1/4 C. vegetable oil
1/4 C. orange juice
1 orange, zest, grated
1/4 C. granulated sugar
3 C. all-purpose flour
2 tsp baking powder

Syrup
1 C. granulated sugar
3/4 C. water
1/2 lemon, juice
1/2 C. honey
oil

Directions
1. In a large bowl, add the flour and baking powder and mix well.
2. In another bowl, add the eggs and beat well.
3. Add the sugar, orange peel, orange juice and oil and beat until well combined.
4. Slowly, add the flour mixture, 1 tbsp at a time and mix until a soft dough forms.
5. With a plastic wrap, cover the bowl and keep aside for about 30 minutes.
6. For the syrup: In a pan, add the sugar, lemon juice and water over medium heat and cook until boiling, stirring continuously.
7. Cook for about 5 minutes.
8. Stir in the honey and cook for about 5 minutes.
9. Remove from the heat and keep aside.
10. Make 10 equal sized balls from the dough and with your hands, flatten each slightly.
11. With your thumbs, create 1-inch hole in the center of each flattened ball.
12. In a deep skillet, add the oil and cook until its temperature reaches to 350 degrees F.
13. Add the doughnuts in batches and cook for about 6 minutes, flipping once half way through.
14. With a slotted spoon, transfer the doughnuts onto a paper towel-lined plate to drain.
15. Coat the warm doughnuts with the sugar and enjoy.
16. With a wooden skewer, prick each warm doughnut in 6-7 places.
17. Coat pricked doughnuts with the warm syrup and enjoy.

Old
German Donuts

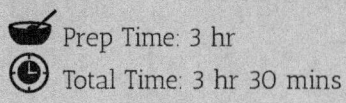

Prep Time: 3 hr
Total Time: 3 hr 30 mins

Servings per Recipe: 40
Calories   114.3
Fat   2.3g
Cholesterol   28.9mg
Sodium   17.1mg
Carbohydrates   19.8g
Protein   3.1g

Ingredients

1 tsp yeast
1 pint milk, scalded and cooled
4 egg yolks
1 egg
1/2 C. sugar
1/4 C. butter
7 C. flour, divided

oil

Directions

1. In a bowl, add the warm milk and yeast and mix until well combined.

2. Add 2 C. of the flour and keep aside in warm area for about 30 minutes.

3. In another bowl, add the eggs and sugar and beat until light.

4. Add the egg mixture into the yeast mixture and mix

5. Add 5 C. of the flour and butter and mx well.

6. Keep aside until doubled in size.

7. Place the dough onto a floured surface and with your hands, pat into 1 1/2-inch thickness.

8. With a doughnut cutter, cut the doughnuts.

9. In a deep skillet, add the oil and cook until its temperature reaches to 350 degrees F.

10. Add the doughnuts in batches and cook until golden brown from both sides.

11. With a slotted spoon, transfer the doughnuts onto a paper towel-lined plate to drain.

12. Coat the warm doughnuts with the sugar and enjoy.

LECHE
Donuts

Prep Time: 20 mins
Total Time: 1 hr 5 mins

Servings per Recipe: 10
Calories   307.6
Fat   6.3g
Cholesterol   76.0mg
Sodium   436.2mg
Carbohydrates   55.1g
Protein   7.2g

Ingredients
3 beaten eggs
1 C. sugar
3 tbsp melted butter
1 tsp salt
1 C. milk
3 1/2 C. sifted flour
4 tsp Watkins baking powder
1 tsp vanilla

1/2 tsp nutmeg

Directions
1. In a bowl, add the flour, baking powder, nutmeg and salt and mix well.
2. Now, sift the flour mixture into a second bowl.
3. In another bowl, add the sugar and eggs and beat well.
4. Add the melted butter and milk and mix until well combined.
5. Add the flour mixture and mix until a soft and light dough forms.
6. Place the dough onto a floured surface and roll into 1/3-inch thickness.
7. With a doughnut cutter, cut the doughnuts.
8. In a deep skillet, add the oil over medium-high heat and cook until heated through.
9. Add the doughnuts in batches and cook until golden brown from both sides.
10. Add the doughnuts in batches and cook for about 3-4 minutes, flipping once half way through.

Evelyn's Cookie Donuts

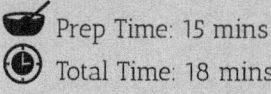 Prep Time: 15 mins

Total Time: 18 mins

Servings per Recipe: 1 batch
Calories	88.1
Fat	2.6g
Cholesterol	18.6mg
Sodium	97.3mg
Carbohydrates	14.0g
Protein	2.1g

Ingredients

1 1/2 C. flour
1 tbsp sugar
1 tsp baking powder
1/4 tsp salt
3/4 C. milk
2 eggs
24 Oreo cookies

oil
powdered sugar

Directions

1. In a bowl, add the flour, baking powder, sugar and salt and mix well.
2. In another bowl, add the eggs and milk and beat well.
3. Add the flour mixture and mix until well combined.
4. Keep aside for about 10 minutes.
5. Now, coat the Oreos with the mixture evenly.
6. In a deep skillet, add the oil and cook until heated through.
7. Add the doughnuts in batches and cook until golden brown from both sides.
8. With a slotted spoon, transfer the doughnuts onto a paper towel-lined plate to drain.
9. Coat the warm doughnuts with the powdered sugar and enjoy.

SAN FRANCISCO
Puffs

Prep Time: 10 mins
Total Time: 13 mins

Servings per Recipe: 1 batch
Calories   571.2
Fat   57.1g
Cholesterol   8.0mg
Sodium   164.6mg
Carbohydrates   14.8g
Protein   1.6g

Ingredients
2 C. flour
3/4 C. sugar, divided
2 tsp baking powder
1/2 tsp baking soda
1 tsp salt
1 tsp ground nutmeg
3/4 C. buttermilk
1 egg

2 tsp cinnamon
6 1/4 C. oil, divided

Directions
1. In a bowl, add the flour, 1/4 C. of the sugar, baking soda, baking powder, nutmeg and salt and mix well.
2. In a second bowl, add the egg, buttermilk and 1/4 C. of the oil and beat until well combined.
3. Add the flour mixture and mix until blended nicely.
4. In a deep skillet, add the oil and cook until its temperature reaches to 375 degrees F.
5. Add the doughnuts in batches and cook for about 2-3 minutes, flipping once half way through.
6. With a slotted spoon, transfer the doughnuts onto a paper towel-lined plate to drain.
7. Coat the warm doughnuts with the cinnamon sugar and enjoy.

15-Minute Donuts

🥣 Prep Time: 10 mins
🕐 Total Time: 15 mins

Servings per Recipe: 1 batch
Calories	154.3
Fat	13.0g
Cholesterol	15.1mg
Sodium	66.9mg
Carbohydrates	8.6g
Protein	0.9g

Ingredients
18 1/4 oz. cake mix, any flavor
1/2 C. flour
4 eggs
1 1/4 C. water
3 C. vegetable oil
1/4 C. confectioners' sugar

Directions

1. In a bowl, add the flour, cake mix, eggs and water and with an electric mixer, beat on low speed for about 5 minutes.
2. In a deep skillet, add the oil and cook until its temperature reaches to 375 degrees F.
3. With a small scooper, add the mixture in batches and cook until golden brown from both sides.
4. Add the doughnuts in batches and cook for about 5 minutes, flipping once half way through.
5. With a slotted spoon, transfer the doughnuts onto a paper towel-lined plate to drain.
6. Sprinkle the warm doughnuts with the confectioners' sugar and enjoy.

HOW TO MAKE
a "Spudnut" (Potato Based Donut)

Prep Time: 20 mins
Total Time: 25 mins

Servings per Recipe: 1 batch
Calories   96.7
Fat   1.0g
Cholesterol   15.0mg
Sodium   130.9mg
Carbohydrates   19.8g
Protein   2.0g

Ingredients
5 C. flour
7 tsp baking powder
1 tsp salt
1 1/2 C. mashed potatoes
3 eggs, well beaten
2 C. granulated sugar
1 1/2 tbsp butter, melted
1 tsp grated nutmeg

1 C. milk
oil

Directions
1. In a bowl, add the flour, baking powder and salt and mix well.
2. Now, sift the flour mixture into a second bowl.
3. In another bowl, add the melted butter, eggs, potatoes and sugar and mix well.
4. Add the milk and nutmeg and mix until well combined.
5. Add the flour mixture and mix until just combined.
6. Refrigerate to chill completely.
7. Place the dough onto a floured surface and roll into 3/8-inch thickness.
8. With a doughnut cutter, cut the doughnuts.
9. In a deep skillet, add the oil and cook until its temperature reaches to 375 degrees F.
10. Add the doughnuts in batches and cook until golden brown from both sides.
11. With a slotted spoon, transfer the doughnuts onto a paper towel-lined plate to drain.
12. Coat the warm doughnuts with the sugar and enjoy.

Cocoa
Spudnuts

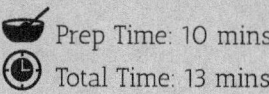 Prep Time: 10 mins
Total Time: 13 mins

Servings per Recipe: 1 batch
Calories	145.4
Fat	2.7g
Cholesterol	23.0mg
Sodium	239.2mg
Carbohydrates	27.5g
Protein	2.8g

Ingredients

1 1/2 C. sugar
1/4 C. melted butter
1 C. cold mashed potatoes
2 eggs, beaten
3 C. flour, sifted
2 tbsp baking powder
1 tsp salt

1 tsp nutmeg
1/2 C. cocoa
1/2 C. buttermilk

Directions

1. In a bowl, add the flour, cocoa powder, baking powder, nutmeg and salt and mix well.
2. Now, sift the flour mixture into a second bowl.
3. In another bowl, add the eggs and beat well.
4. Add the potatoes, sugar and butter and beat until creamy.
5. Add the flour mixture, alternating with the milk and ix until well combined.
6. Refrigerate for whole night.
7. Place the dough onto a floured surface and roll into 1/2-inch thickness.
8. With a doughnut cutter, cut the doughnuts.
9. In a deep skillet, add the oil and cook until its temperature reaches to 365 degrees F.
10. Add the doughnuts in batches and cook for about 3 minutes, flipping once half way through.
11. With a slotted spoon, transfer the doughnuts onto a paper towel-lined plate to drain.
12. Coat the warm doughnuts with the sugar and enjoy.

ALLEGANY
Donut Squares

Prep Time: 15 mins
Total Time: 21 mins

Servings per Recipe: 1 batch
Calories	3473.1
Fat	65.0g
Cholesterol	228.5mg
Sodium	2780.8mg
Carbohydrates	691.7g
Protein	49.9g

Ingredients

1 (1/4 oz.) package granular yeast
1/2 C. lukewarm water
1 tsp sugar
1/2 C. scalded milk
1/4 C. sugar
1/4 C. shortening
1 tsp salt
1 tsp cinnamon
1 C. raisins

1 egg
2 1/2-2 3/4 C. unsifted all-purpose flour, divided
Glaze
2 tbsp honey
1/8 tsp salt
2 C. icing sugar
7 tbsp boiling water

Directions

1. In a bowl, add 1/2 C. lukewarm water 1 tsp of the sugar and mix well.
2. Add the yeast and gently, stir.
3. Keep aside for about 10 minutes.
4. Meanwhile, in bowl, add the shortening, raisins, 1/4 C. of the sugar, cinnamon and salt and mix until well combined.
5. Keep aside until cool to lukewarm.
6. Add egg and beat until well combined.
7. Add the yeast mixture and 2 1/4 C. of the flour and beat for about 5 minutes.
8. With a plastic wrap, cover the bowl and keep aside in a warm area for about 2 hours.
9. With your hands, punch down the dough.
10. Now, place the dough onto a floured surface with the remaining flour and with your hands, knead for about 10 minutes.
11. Roll the dough into 1/3-inch thickness and then, cut into 3 inch squares.
12. Keep aside, uncovered for at least 1 1/2 hours.
13. In a deep skillet, add the oil and cook until its temperature reaches to 375 degrees F.
14. Add the doughnuts in batches and cook for about 1 1/2 minutes, flipping once half way through.
15. With a slotted spoon, transfer the doughnuts onto a paper towel-lined plate to drain.
16. Meanwhile, for the glaze: in a bowl, add all the ingredients and mix until smooth.
17. Coat the warm doughnuts with the glaze and enjoy.

Coconut
Glazed Banana Donuts

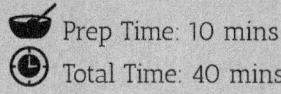 Prep Time: 10 mins

Total Time: 40 mins

Servings per Recipe: 12
Calories   1313.8
Fat   113.4g
Cholesterol   0.0mg
Sodium   96.0mg
Carbohydrates   73.5g
Protein   4.2g

Ingredients
3 1/2 C. flour
1 1/3 C. sugar
2 tsp baking powder
2 ripe bananas, mashed
1 tbsp vanilla
1 1/2 C. water
1/4 C. crushed pineapple
6 C. oil

cinnamon-sugar mixture
Syrup
1/3 C. water
1/3 C. sugar
1 C. coconut milk
1/8 tsp sea salt
1 tsp vanilla

Directions
1. In a bowl, add the flour, baking powder and sugar and mix well.
2. Add the pineapple, bananas, water and vanilla extract and mix until a sticky dough forms.
3. In a deep skillet, add 3-inch deep oil and cook until its temperature reaches to 350 degrees F.
4. With a scooper, add the mixture in batches and cook until golden brown from both sides.
5. With a slotted spoon, transfer the doughnuts onto a paper towel-lined plate to drain.
6. Coat the warm doughnuts with the cinnamon sugar and enjoy.

AKRON
Drop Donuts

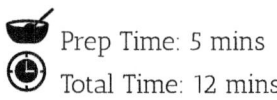 Prep Time: 5 mins
Total Time: 12 mins

Servings per Recipe: 1 batch
Calories	901.5
Fat	21.3g
Cholesterol	79.0mg
Sodium	998.9mg
Carbohydrates	161.7g
Protein	14.7g

Ingredients
1 (18 1/4 oz.) packages wild blueberry
muffin mix
1/2 C. flour
3/4 C. milk
1 egg
shortening
1/2 C. sugar
1 tsp cinnamon

Directions
1. In a bowl, add the flour and muffin mix and mix well.
2. Add the egg and milk and egg and mix until just combined.
3. Add the blueberries and gently, stir to combine.
4. In a deep skillet, add the shortening and cook until its temperature reaches to 365 degrees F.
5. With tsp, add the mixture in batches and cook until golden brown from both sides.
6. With a slotted spoon, transfer the doughnuts onto a paper towel-lined plate to drain.
7. Meanwhile, in a bowl, add the cinnamon and sugar and mix well.
8. Coat the warm doughnuts with the cinnamon sugar and enjoy.

Caribbean
Air Donuts

Prep Time: 15 mins
Total Time: 15 mins

Servings per Recipe: 1 batch
Calories   34.3
Fat   0.7g
Cholesterol   0.0mg
Sodium   20.7mg
Carbohydrates   6.1g
Protein   0.7g

Ingredients
2 C. all-purpose flour
2 tsp baking powder
2 tbsp sugar
1/2 C. thick coconut milk
powdered sugar

Directions
1. In a bowl, add all the ingredients and mix until a dough forms.
2. Place the dough onto a floured surface and roll into 1/3-inch thickness.
3. Cut the rolled dough into long strips and then cut into diamonds.
4. In a deep skillet, add the oil and cook until heated through.
5. Add the dough diamonds in batches and cook until golden brown from both sides.
6. With a slotted spoon, transfer the dough diamonds onto a paper towel-lined plate to drain.
7. Coat the warm doughnuts with the powdered sugar and enjoy.

MATZO
Donuts

🥣 Prep Time: 20 mins

🕐 Total Time: 1 hr 20 mins

Servings per Recipe: 20
Calories	83.6
Fat	6.2g
Cholesterol	31.7mg
Sodium	41.3mg
Carbohydrates	5.3g
Protein	1.4g

Ingredients
2/3 C. water
1 tbsp sugar
1/4 tsp salt
1/2 C. oil
1 C. matzo meal
3 eggs
cinnamon-sugar mixture
chopped nuts

Directions
1. Set your oven to 375 degrees F before doing anything else and grease a baking sheet.
2. In a pan, add the oil, water, sugar and salt and cook until boiling.
3. Add the matzo meal and stir to combine.
4. Remove from the heat and keep aside to cool slightly.
5. Add the eggs, one at a time, beating well after each addition.
6. With greased hands, make 2-inch balls from the dough.
7. Sprinkle the top of each ball with the cinnamon sugar and nuts.
8. In the bottom of the prepared baking sheet, arrange the dough balls.
9. Cook in the oven for about 1 hour.
10. Enjoy warm.

True American Donut

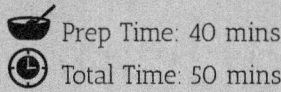 Prep Time: 40 mins

Total Time: 50 mins

Servings per Recipe: 1 batch
Calories	68.4
Fat	1.1g
Cholesterol	8.9mg
Sodium	101.5mg
Carbohydrates	13.2g
Protein	1.3g

Ingredients

7 1/2 C. sugar
3/4 C. lard
9 eggs
3 (8 oz.) cans evaporated milk
3 (8 oz.) cans water
18 C. flour
18 tsp baking powder

7 1/2 tsp salt
9 tsp nutmeg

Directions

1. In a bowl, add the flour, baking powder, nutmeg and salt and mix well.
2. Now, sift the flour mixture into another bowl.
3. In another bowl, add the lard and sugar and beat until creamy.
4. Add the eggs and beat until well combined.
5. Add the evaporated milk and water and beat until well combined.
6. Add the flour mixture and mix until a stiff dough forms.
7. Place the dough onto a floured surface and roll into 1/2-inch thickness.
8. With a doughnut cutter, cut the doughnuts.
9. In a deep skillet, add the oil and cook until heated through.
10. Add the doughnuts in batches and cook until golden brown from both sides.
11. With a slotted spoon, transfer the doughnuts onto a paper towel-lined plate to drain.
12. Enjoy warm.

CINNAMON
Wedding Donuts

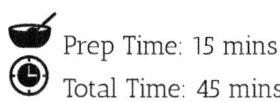 Prep Time: 15 mins

Total Time: 45 mins

Servings per Recipe: 36

Calories	65.4
Fat	0.9g
Cholesterol	12.4mg
Sodium	91.3mg
Carbohydrates	13.1g
Protein	1.2g

Ingredients

2 C. flour
3/4 C. sugar
2 tsp baking powder
3/4 C. milk
1 tsp salt
2 eggs, beaten
1 tsp vanilla
1 tbsp shortening, melted

1/4 tsp nutmeg
1/4 tsp cinnamon
1 C. confectioners' sugar
2 tbsp water

Directions

1. Set your oven to 325 degrees F before doing anything else and lightly, grease a mini doughnut pan.
2. In a bowl, add the flour, baking powder, sugar and salt and mix well.
3. Add the milk, eggs, shortening and vanilla and beat until well combined.
4. In the prepared doughnut holes, place the mixture about 2/3 full.
5. Cook in the oven for about 8 minutes.
6. Remove from the oven and keep aside to cool.
7. For the glaze: in a bowl, add the confectioners' sugar, nutmeg, cinnamon and water and beat until well combined
8. Carefully, remove the doughnuts from the pan.
9. Coat with the glaze and enjoy.

Virginia
Corn Donuts

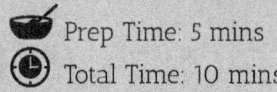

Prep Time: 5 mins
Total Time: 10 mins

Servings per Recipe: 1 batch
Calories   205.2
Fat   4.4g
Cholesterol   30.9mg
Sodium   408.0mg
Carbohydrates   36.4g
Protein   4.4g

Ingredients
2 2/3 C. all-purpose flour
1 (8 1/2 oz.) boxes Jiffy corn muffin mix
3/4 C. sugar
1 tsp baking soda
1 tsp salt
2 eggs
1/2 C. sour cream
1/2 C. milk
1 tsp vanilla
vegetable oil
cinnamon sugar

Directions
1. In a bowl, add the flour, corn muffin mix, sugar, baking soda and salt and mix well.
2. Add the eggs, sour cream, milk and vanilla and mix well.
3. Place the dough onto a corn meal lined smooth surface and with your hands, pat into 1/2-inch thickness.
4. Then, cut the dough into 16 equal sized strips.
5. Shape the dough strips into doughnut circles.
6. In a deep skillet, add the oil and cook until its temperature reaches to 325 degrees F.
7. Add the doughnuts in batches and cook for about 30-40 seconds, flipping once half way through.
8. With a slotted spoon, transfer the doughnuts onto a paper towel-lined plate to drain.
9. Coat the warm doughnuts with the cinnamon sugar and enjoy.

GERMAN
Cream Filled Donuts

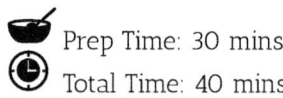

Prep Time: 30 mins
Total Time: 40 mins

Servings per Recipe: 18
Calories	152.1
Fat	9.7g
Cholesterol	52.4mg
Sodium	34.9mg
Carbohydrates	13.6g
Protein	2.4g

Ingredients

1 package active dry yeast
1/4 C. warm water
1/2 C. whipping cream
1/3 C. softened butter
2 tbsp sugar
1 egg
2 C. all-purpose flour
Cream Filling

2/3 C. whipping cream
1 tbsp all-purpose flour
1 tbsp sugar
1 tsp vanilla
1 egg yolk
hot fat
powdered sugar

Directions

1. In a bowl, add the warm water and yeast and mix until well combined.
2. Keep aside for about 5 minutes.
3. Add the butter, whipping cream, egg and sugar and beat until well combined.
4. Add 1 C. of the flour and whisk until smooth.
5. Slowly, add the remaining flour and whisk until smooth.
6. With a plastic wrap, cover the bowl and keep aside for about 30 minutes.
7. Again beat until smooth.
8. Keep aside for about 30 minutes.
9. Meanwhile, for the filling: in a heavy-bottomed pot, add all the ingredients over medium heat and cook until boiling.
10. Cook for about 5 minutes, stirring frequently.
11. Remove from the heat and keep aside to cool.
12. Place the dough onto a lightly floured surface.
13. Make a ball from the dough and then, roll into an 18-inch square.
14. Place the filling onto half of the dough about 3 inches apart.
15. Fold other half of the dough over the filling.
16. With a C., cut the cakes and with your fingers, press the edges to seal.

17. Place the puffs onto a lightly floured piece of waxed paper and keep aside for about 30 - 40 minutes.
18. In a deep skillet, add the oil and cook until its temperature reaches to 375 degrees F.
19. Add the doughnuts in batches and cook until golden brown from both sides.
20. With a slotted spoon, transfer the doughnuts onto a paper towel - lined plate to drain.
21. Coat the warm doughnuts with the powdered sugar and enjoy.

DOUGHNUTS
Leviathan

Prep Time: 1 hr 30 mins
Total Time: 1 hr 32 mins

Servings per Recipe: 24
Calories	224.4
Fat	5.4g
Cholesterol	17.6mg
Sodium	201.3mg
Carbohydrates	38.3g
Protein	5.0g

Ingredients
3/4 C. sugar
1/2 C. oil
2 (1/4 oz.) package yeast
2 eggs, beaten
2 tsp salt
3 C. water
1 tsp nutmeg
8 C. flour

Directions
1. In a bowl, add 1 C. of the warm water and yeast and mix well.
2. In another bowl, add the oil, 2 C. of the hot water, eggs, some flour, sugar, nutmeg and salt and mix until well combined.
3. Add the remaining flour and yeast mixture and mix until well combined.
4. With a plastic wrap, cover the bowl and keep aside in a warm area for about 1 1/2 hours.
5. Place the dough onto a floured surface and roll into 1/2-inch thickness.
6. With a doughnut cutter, cut the doughnuts.
7. In the bottom of 2 floured baking sheets, arrange the doughnuts and keep aside in a warm area for about 30 minutes.
8. In a deep skillet, add the oil and cook until heated through.
9. Add the doughnuts in batches and cook until golden brown from both sides.
10. With a slotted spoon, transfer the doughnuts onto a paper towel-lined plate to drain.
11. Enjoy warm.

Doughnuts
Saskatoon Saskatchewan

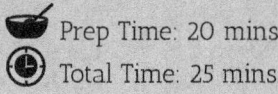 Prep Time: 20 mins

Total Time: 25 mins

Servings per Recipe: 1 batch
Calories   248.9
Fat   2.6g
Cholesterol   36.1mg
Sodium   403.8mg
Carbohydrates   50.0g
Protein   6.1g

Ingredients

2 C. sugar
2 tsp salt
6 tbsp corn oil
4 eggs
2 1/4 C. buttermilk
8 C. flour
8 tsp baking powder

1 tsp baking soda
1 pinch ginger
1 tsp nutmeg

Directions

1. In a bowl, add all the ingredients and mix until well combined.
2. Place the dough onto a floured surface and with your hands, kneed until a non-sticky dough forms.
3. With a rolling pin, roll the dough into 1/4-inch thickness.
4. With a doughnut cutter, cut the doughnuts.
5. In a deep skillet, add the oil and cook until its temperature reaches to 400 degrees F.
6. Add the doughnuts in batches and cook until golden brown from both sides.
7. With a slotted spoon, transfer the doughnuts onto a paper towel-lined plate to drain.
8. Enjoy warm.

SOUTHERN
Donut Pudding

Prep Time: 20 mins
Total Time: 2 hr 20 mins

Servings per Recipe: 20
Calories	453.1
Fat	23.0g
Cholesterol	149.5mg
Sodium	304.3mg
Carbohydrates	53.0g
Protein	9.3g

Ingredients
20 stale plain doughnuts, chopped
1 quart milk
12 eggs, beaten
2 C. sugar
1 tbsp sugar
1/2 C. raisins
2 tbsp vanilla
4 oz. butter

1 tbsp cinnamon

Directions
1. Set your oven to 350 degrees F before doing anything else.
2. In a bowl, add the milk and eggs and beat until well combined.
3. Add the sugar, doughnuts, raisins and vanilla and gently, stir to combine.
4. In another bowl, add the cinnamon and sugar and mix well.
5. In 2 (9x13-inch) baking dishes, divide the mixture evenly.
6. Arrange the butter slices on top and dust with the cinnamon sugar.
7. With the pieces of foil, cover the baking dishes.
8. Cook in the oven for about 1 hour.
9. Remove the foil pieces and cook for about 45-60 minutes.
10. Enjoy.

Doughnuts
Brasileiro

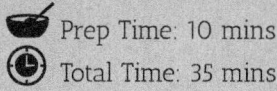

Prep Time: 10 mins
Total Time: 35 mins

Servings per Recipe: 1 batch
Calories   37.3
Fat   0.6g
Cholesterol   15.5mg
Sodium   130.6mg
Carbohydrates   6.5g
Protein   1.2g

Ingredients

1 C. all-purpose flour
1/2 C. cornstarch
2 tsp baking powder
1/2 C. milk
2 eggs
2-3 green onions, chopped
1 tsp salt

oil

Directions

1. In a bowl, add the corn starch, flour and baking powder and mix well.
2. In another bowl, add the eggs, green onions and salt and beat well.
3. Add the flour mixture, alternating with the milk and mix until a thick mixture is formed.
4. In a deep skillet, add the oil and cook until its temperature reaches to 350 degrees F.
5. With a tbsp, add the mixture in batches and cook for about 3-4 minutes, flipping once half way through.
6. With a slotted spoon, transfer the doughnuts onto a paper towel-lined plate to drain.
7. Enjoy warm.

SPANISH
Doughnuts

Prep Time: 1 hr 30 mins
Total Time: 2 hr

Servings per Recipe: 1 batch
Calories	791.8
Fat	20.0g
Cholesterol	245.1mg
Sodium	472.4mg
Carbohydrates	125.4g
Protein	25.3g

Ingredients
2 (1/4 oz.) packhge each active dry yeast
1/2 C. warm water
1 1/2 C. warm milk
5 eggs, beaten
5 tbsp sugar
1/4 C. butter, softened
1/2 tsp salt
5 - 5 1/2 C. all-purpose flour

oil
granulated sugar

Directions
1. In a bowl, add the warm water and yeast and mix until well combined.
2. Add the butter, milk, eggs, sugar and salt and beat until smooth.
3. Add enough flour and mix until a soft dough forms.
4. In a greased bowl, place the dough and turn to coat the top.
5. With a plastic wrap, cover the bowl and keep aside in a warm area for about 1 hour.
6. In a deep skillet, add the oil and cook until its temperature reaches to 375 degrees F.
7. With a tbsp, add the mixture and cook for about 3-4 minutes, flipping once half way through.
8. With a slotted spoon, transfer the doughnuts onto a paper towel-lined plate to drain.
9. Coat the warm doughnuts with the granulated sugar and enjoy.

Classical
Herman Doughnuts I

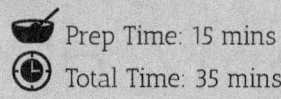 Prep Time: 15 mins
Total Time: 35 mins

Servings per Recipe: 12
Calories	289 kcal
Carbohydrates	26.1 g
Cholesterol	32 mg
Fat	19.1 g
Fiber	0.6 g
Protein	3.5 g
Sodium	218 mg

Ingredients
8 cups vegetable oil (for frying)
3 tbsps shortening
1/2 cup white sugar
2 eggs, beaten
1 cup Herman Sourdough Starter
1/2 cup milk
2 cups all-purpose flour
1 tsp baking soda
1/2 tsp salt
1/4 tsp ground nutmeg
2 tbsps confectioners' sugar

Directions
1. Get a bowl, mix: sugar and shortening, milk and Herman starter (make a cream).
2. Get a 2nd bowl, mix: nutmeg, flour, and baking soda.
3. Combine both bowls, knead, to form dough.
4. Add flour to a countertop for rolling out the dough.
5. Roll dough to a thickness of 1/4 of an inch cut with doughnut cutter.
6. Let doughnuts sit for 1 hour while covered to rise.
7. Get a deep fryer. Set oil to 375 degrees.
8. Fry doughnuts in batches for 1 min per side.
9. Remove from oil. Drain excess.
10. Enjoy.

A DOUGHNUT
from Cake Mix

Prep Time: 2 hr
Total Time: 2 hr 15 mins

Servings per Recipe: 1 batch
Calories   257 kcal
Carbohydrates   28.6 g
Cholesterol   20 mg
Fat   14.7 g
Fiber   0.7 g
Protein   3 g
Sodium   167 mg

Ingredients

2 1/2 cups all-purpose flour
1/2 cup white sugar
1 tbsp baking powder
1/2 tsp salt
1 tsp ground cinnamon
1/4 tsp ground nutmeg
1 cup milk
1 egg, beaten

1/4 cup butter, melted and cooled
2 tsps vanilla extract
2 quarts oil for deep frying
1/2 tsp ground cinnamon
1/2 cup white sugar

Directions

1. Get a bowl, mix: nutmeg, flour, cinnamon, 1/2 cup of sugar, salt, and baking powder.

2. Create an opening in the center, add: vanilla, milk, butter, and egg.

3. Combine form dough. Cover and let rise hour in the frig.

4. Get a deep fryer. Set oil to 375 degrees.

5. Roll dough on floured surface to a thickness of 1/4 of an inch cut with doughnut cutter.

6. Fry until completely golden. Set aside and remove excess oils.

7. Coat doughnuts with: half a cup of sugar, and half a cup of cinnamon, combined.

8. Serving Size: 16 doughnuts and holes.

Strawberry Shortcake Sweet Doughnut

Prep Time: 15 mins
Total Time: 15 mins

Servings per Recipe: 4
Calories   766 kcal
Carbohydrates   57.4 g
Cholesterol   167 mg
Fat   58.2 g
Fiber   3.8 g
Protein   7.3 g
Sodium   252 m

Ingredients

2 cups heavy whipping cream
1/2 cup confectioners' sugar
1 tsp vanilla extract
4 glazed doughnuts, halved horizontally
1 quart strawberries, hulled and sliced

Directions

1. Get a bowl, mix: vanilla extract, cream, and sugar.
2. Use electric mixer to form whipped cream.
3. Take one doughnut and cut it in half. Top with ¼ cup of cream.
4. Top cream with ¼ cup of strawberries.
5. Top with remaining doughnut half. Continue for remaining doughnuts.
6. Enjoy.

ENJOY THE RECIPES?

KEEP ON COOKING
WITH 6 MORE FREE COOKBOOKS!

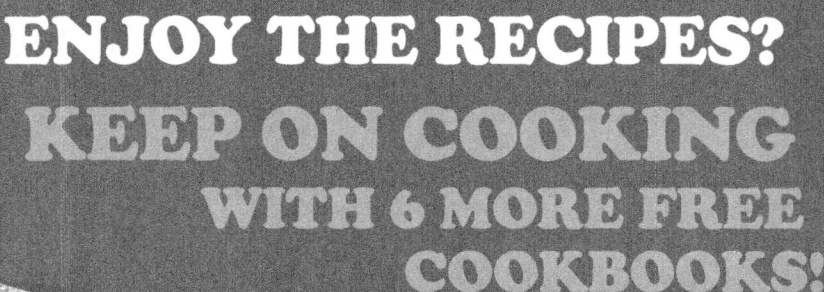

Visit our website and simply enter your email address to join the club and receive your 6 cookbooks.

http://booksumo.com/magnet

Printed in Great Britain
by Amazon

24287271R00057